The Spark of Faith

Fr. Wojciech Giertych, OP

The Spark of Faith

Understanding the Power of Reaching Out to God

EWTN PUBLISHING, INC.
Irondale, Alabama

Cover design by Perceptions Design Studio.

The Spark of Faith is an English translation of *Rozruch wiary* (Pelplin, Poland: Wydawnictwo Bernardinum, 2012).

Scripture quotations have been taken from the *The Jerusalem Bible* (London: Eyre and Spottiswoode, 1968).

Nihil obstat: Fr. Zdzisław Benedict, Censor Librorum
Imprimatur: Wiesław Śmigiel, Bishop of Pelplin
September 28, 2012, L.dz. 1089/2021/IA

The "Nihil Obstat" and "Imprimatur" are official declarations that a book or pamphlet is free of doctrinal or moral error. No implication is contained therein that those who have granted the Nihil Obstat and the Imprimatur agree with the content, opinions or statements expressed.

EWTN Publishing, Inc.
5817 Old Leeds Road, Irondale, AL 35210

Distributed by Sophia Institute Press, Box 5284, Manchester, NH 03108.

Library of Congress Cataloging-in-Publication Data

Names: Giertych, Wojciech, 1951- author.
Title: The Spark of Faith Understanding the Power of Reaching Out to God / Fr. Wojciech Giertych, OP.
Other titles: Rozruch wiary. English
Description: Ironadale, Alabama : EWTN Publishing, Inc., 2018. | Includes bibliographical references.
Identifiers: LCCN 2018016502 | ISBN 9781682780688 (pbk. : alk. paper)
Subjects: LCSH: Faith. | Catholic Church—Doctrines.
Classification: LCC BT771.3 .G5313 2018 | DDC 234/.23—dc23 LC record available at https://lccn.loc.gov/2018016502

First printing

Contents

Preface to the English Edition

This book was written with a pastoral intent. It was designed as a helpful tool for a spiritual living out of the Year of Faith announced by Pope Benedict XVI. As such, this is not a work of academic theology filled with quotations and references. Watchful readers may easily recognize the sources of my presentation. I have no reason to hide them; in fact, I am deeply indebted to those who have gone before me and have led me to understand the importance of faith. Among them, first of all, I have to mention St. Thomas Aquinas, whose treatise on faith in the *Summa Theologiae* remains a standard point of reference. Second, there is the youngest Doctor of the Church, St. Thérèse of Lisieux, whose writings offer a wonderful practical schooling in faith. And then, there are several theologians, whose works I have read and used in my teaching and preaching over the years. The first one that I have to mention is the French Carmelite Fr. Marie-Eugène of the Child Jesus. (Recently, he was beatified in Avignon.) Further theological masters include Fr. Michel Labourdette, OP, a long-time professor of moral theology in Toulouse. His mimeographed notes on the *IIa pars* of the *Summa Theologiae*, in which, article after article, he explains the doctrine of Aquinas, are the best commentary on the *Summa* that I have ever found.[1] I have followed his notes in my courses at the Roman Angelicum. Another master whom, years back, I was urged to read is Fr. Marie-Joseph Le Guillou, OP. I have found a profound light in his books showing the importance of doing theology in unison with the spiritual life. And finally, I need to mention Fr. Servais Pinckaers, OP, and to thank him for his liberating vision of the fundamentals of Christian morals.

This book is derivative, very much based on the works of the above masters, whom I have closely followed, without always specifying from whom I have drawn. Wherever I have been inexact or have simplified issues, the fault is mine. But there was a reason for this: All theological thinking is located in some specific context. I wrote this book in Polish, thinking about the needs of the average Catholic in Poland, who is generally put off by academic theological works. Recently, while reading about Latin American theology, I noticed a similarity with Polish Catholicism. Where Catholic identity is drawn from a surrounding culture marked by post-Tridentine theology and piety, thinking about faith is not a prime concern, because it seems to be automatic. This is unfortunate, because then faith, while respected and unquestioned, has little practical impact on lives. Furthermore, this world is marked by a profound rift that dates from the Enlightenment, though its roots can be traced to Baroque theology. Reason seems to be skeptical and disdaining of faith, while faith is seen to be a sentimental, emotional affair tied with popular devotions. Catholic society in such countries is torn within between the intellectuals who are critical of popular

[1] Michel Labourdette, OP, *Cours de la théologie morale : La foi IIa-IIae, qq. 1–16* (Toulouse, 1959–1960).

religiosity and the masses who feel that they are being scorned. The consequence is that despite the common Catholic background there are deep social conflicts, little true thinking within faith and about faith, and almost no concern for the deepening of faith's rooting in the soul. Catholic intellectuals are tempted to bypass theology and to focus primarily on philosophy, as if trying to serve faith from without, while pastors are tempted to maintain religious traditions only in a mechanical way and to focus primarily on social and political issues, seeing in them the major danger. In both these approaches, the perception of the supernatural character of faith and its inherent forces of growth seems to be lost. That is why in my book, I am trying to combat both the Gnostic elevation of reason above faith and the Semi-Pelagian treatment of faith as a quality acquired through natural effort and in response to some externally imposed obligation. Writing for the Polish Church, I saw the need of insisting repeatedly and directly upon this throughout the book.

Catholics in the English-speaking world, and also in France, are more directly concerned about their faith and Catholic identity. They know that they have to struggle to maintain it, because it is not automatic. Thus they are searching for assistance in the deepening of their faith and in the structuring of a synthesis of their cultural and moral life within faith. This book may therefore seem to them to speak about things that seem obvious. Nevertheless, at the request of my students I have translated it into English, hoping that it may be useful as it reminds us that faith has within itself the capacity to spark the supernatural life in the soul.

As I present this book, I have to thank Luanne Zurlo, who has urged me to translate it and then carefully corrected my translation, pointing out where my turns of phrases and simplifications require a reformulation in view of American reactions. This has been an enormous help, making this book more readable. I also thank Charles McKinney and the editors from EWTN Publishing Inc. for their helpful and necessary linguistic and grammatical corrections.

The Vatican, June 29, 2017
Solemnity of St. Peter and St. Paul

The Spark of Faith

Introduction

Faith is a divine gift that enables the encounter with God. It is the first impulse of the supernatural life in the human soul. When there is a moment of faith, when the believer consciously focuses the mind toward God, in view of Himself, there is a direct contact with the mysterious but living God. From this moment, the divine life is present in the individual and is set in motion. Throughout the time that a person persists in a lively faith, he is animated from within by divine grace. When he breaks this contact with God—when an obstacle has been erected between him and God—divine grace is excluded from the soul, and so it cannot transform the soul from within. Only a reiterated impulse of divine grace, one that is given freely and gratuitously, will restore that lively faith, and it will allow for a renewed encounter with God in faith and love.

This book is not addressed to unbelievers, but to those who already have faith and want to deepen it and to understand it, and also to those who want to help others along in that process. So, this book does not have an apologetic purpose. It is not trying to prove that belief in God is useful, or to disprove the notion that belief in God is absurd. It does not attempt to persuade unbelievers so that, despite everything, they will allow themselves to be convinced about faith. It takes for granted what the Church teaches: Faith is a gift of grace, given by God. It is not trying to suggest that some human arguments, even those that are logically sound, have the power to lead somebody to faith. This book is addressed to those who already believe and who want to look into their faith, because they sense that faith is important. They want to sort out their thinking about faith in a way that is in accord with the Church's teaching, so as to grasp what faith is, what its function is, how it may expand in the soul, and how, unfortunately, it may also wither.

Since faith is a divine gift, it is a precious gift that should not be ignored. Since it is a gift that is alive, we can look into the laws of its development. Since it may grow but also wane, we need to know the principles of its nourishment so that it will not die out but, rather, will fulfill the function that God, its Giver, has assigned to it. It is important to see how faith may be deepened, how it may influence the intellectual and moral life. Faith, after all, is not a dead but valuable object that one simply possesses and locks up for safety in a vault. Faith is given by God together with hope and charity, the love that is divine, so that we may live out these theological virtues. Faith, which is the first gift, gets the other virtues going, and these then have an impact on the entire moral life.

The most important thing that we have to say about faith is that it is the overpowering of the human spirit by God, Who, as the First and most fundamental Truth, sets and focuses the mind and the will toward Himself. As a result, the living dynamism of God Himself appears in the human soul. This is a basic fact about true faith, whether it is the faith of a baptized infant, the faith of a child receiving First Holy Communion, the faith of man immersed in sin but crying out toward God, or the faith of an advanced mystic experiencing a profound purification of faith. It is from this fundamental fact that everything else that we will later say about faith derives.

Faith does not destroy reason, so it does not prevent the mind from asking questions and attempting to know everything, including the supernatural reality. But even for the believing person, faith always remains a mystery. Human reason, therefore, may ponder faith, may look into it, and may try to define it and to describe it. Looking into faith may begin with human experience. It will then view the psyche of the believing person, trying to identify the essential elements of the process of belief. Such a cognitive approach is theoretically possible, but by no means is it easy. In fact, it is easier to pinpoint the fundamental characteristics of a deformed faith than those of a true faith. We can perceive with greater facility the specifics of a sentimental faith, the faith of a bigot, or the faith of a fundamentalist, than faith *itself*. The empirical sciences, including psychology, do not possess tools that would enable the cognition of a supernatural reality.

The study of faith may also try to begin with a sociological description. Most often, however, such inquiries stop short of viewing faith itself, and instead observe *religiosity*. This is an interesting theme that engages sociologists, ethnographers, and journalists, but it is not an examination of faith itself. Grasping faith itself and its laws of development in the soul requires a theological approach. Here the point of departure is the truth as it has been revealed by God Himself. Once it is accepted, then, through the effort of the believing mind, it may be precisely articulated.

Revelation tells us that "faith is the assurance of things hoped for, the conviction of things not seen" (Heb. 11:1). In Catholic tradition this sentence is treated as a sort of explanation of the essence of faith. It is not easy to translate. It points out that in faith there is a received content that corresponds with the aspirations of the believer's spirit and warrants them, and, furthermore, that faith is the source of a conviction that is based not upon the obviousness of the nature of things but on the authority of God. This sentence has to be read in unison with many other data of revelation that describe faith and lead to it. In the Gospels, Jesus always awaited faith in men and women, and without it He could not do any miracles. Faith is not only an epistemological fact, in which, for some reason, that which is not evident is accepted. Above all, faith is an indispensable receptacle of the "spring of water welling up to eternal life" (John 4:14). For a true life of faith and for its growth, it is this moment that needs to be emphasized. The Church has no doubt that it is through the power of faith that we receive grace flowing from the open heart of Jesus. "He who saw it has borne witness—his testimony is true, and he knows that he tells the truth—that you also may believe" (John 19:35).

In preparation for the Year of Faith
The Vatican, June 3, 2012
Trinity Sunday

1

Why Is Faith Important?

Faith is an indispensable tool

"Without faith … it is impossible to please God. Anyone who comes to him must believe that He exists and that He rewards those who earnestly seek him" (Heb. 11:6). Contact with God is always made through faith. God is not a philosophical fact, known uniquely through an autonomous reason seeking after truth. He is a living God, a personal God, and so He awaits a personal human response. A lively, authentic relationship with Him and the maintenance of that relationship requires a special disposition, completely different from a cognitive curiosity, which can be satisfied by natural thinking arriving at the truth, by looking into an encyclopedia, or through a sudden brain wave. We may accomplish a great deal by our own powers. We can get to know the world, undertake various sciences, and work with more or less success toward some chosen good or evil ends. Using our reason we may even come to the conclusion that some divine being must exist, as the final justification for the world around us and its order, some Absolute that is its final end. But the fact remains that we cannot actually learn very much about God by our own powers. We cannot have a relationship with Him, or, for that matter, we cannot by ourselves develop a friendship with Him or become the recipients of His special, supernatural gifts. For this to happen, or, even more, for the friendly meeting and encounter with God to happen frequently, a kind of realignment needs to occur within us, and this can be accomplished only by God Himself. It is He who draws us toward Himself and who grants us a supernatural capacity. It is only because of this that we are able to meet God, revealed as Father, Son, and Holy Spirit; it is only because of this that we can begin to know ourselves as His child, and to open ourselves up to His particular gifts. God eagerly shares His love, His inner life, which we call the grace of the Holy Spirit. This grace, received, renewed, and recognized as decisive, completely transforms human life.

Faith, which makes our meeting with God possible, is a divine gift, but its actualization depends on us. As it is received, faith can be expressed in the heart. The believer may use it, may agree that it gives him a fundamental orientation in life, but he may also choose to ignore it, and even to extinguish it completely. In the Gospels we see that Jesus always expected from people a living faith directed at Him. Without this He could not perform miracles (see Mark 6:1–6). Faith was always an absolutely necessary condition for the effusion of His graces. When in place of it there was indifference, or worse, repugnance, or when people tried to put Jesus to the test, this became a sort of wall blocking Jesus' spontaneous and automatic readiness to share His divine power. But when the thief, hanging on the cross for his true crimes, recognized through faith—because, after all, this could not have been an empirical discovery—that Jesus is the Messiah sent by God, immediately he received the promise of eternal life in paradise (Luke 23:39–43). Similarly, the woman suffering from a hemorrhage, treated for this reason as impure, who boldly made her way through the crowd and touched the hem of Jesus' cloak with her finger, and, even more, touched Him with her faith, was immediately healed. In turn, Jesus realized that power had come out of Him (Mark 5:21–34).

Every outpouring of grace, made possible by active human faith removing the divide between man and God, is a moment of great joy for the Holy Trinity, because "there is more joy in giving than in receiving" (Acts 20:35). In such moments, Jesus rejoiced in the Holy Spirit, glorifying the Father, who hid these things from the wise and learned, and revealed them to the simple (Luke 10:21). Jesus expected faith everywhere, and not just the kind that is expressed occasionally, but the kind that is lasting and sustained and that lets Him rejoice in the lavish and generous pouring out of His power. Before sending the apostles out for the last time, Jesus chastised them for their "lack of faith and their stubborn refusal to believe those who had seen Him after He had risen," and announced that "whoever believes and is baptized will be saved, but whoever does not believe will be condemned" (Mark 16:14, 16).

The formation of the disciples' faith

As Jesus was forming his disciples, there were many instances they remembered as a true initiation in the school of faith. As they were in a boat on the lake, with Jesus asleep and thus seemingly completely absent, a violent wind came upon them, and they began to panic. When they finally woke Jesus up, He immediately calmed the gale and "there was a great silence." Jesus then reprimanded them for their lack of faith (Mark 4:35–41). This scene demonstrates the power of faith, which can calm waves and restless emotions and grants an interior order opening up to God. At another instance Jesus walked on water in order to teach the disciples that in the most important things in life and in their ministry they have to have the courage to base themselves not on that which is sure, as the tenets of physics are sure, but on the mystery of faith, which requires going out further, past the limits of human reasoning, even though, of course, this can generate trepidation. This grounding of oneself in faith is also certain, but it is a different kind of certitude, which has its source in the promise of grace. When Peter took the risk of walking on water, he was able to walk toward Jesus so long as he believed in Him. But the moment Peter doubted, he began to sink (Matt. 14:22–31).

In the Gospel of John we have recorded two notable dialogues, which perhaps had been edited by the Evangelist with the thought of preparing catechumens for Baptism. These two dialogues show the supernatural pedagogy that Jesus uses to lead people to a living faith.

The first dialogue is between Jesus and Nicodemus. The conversation initially seemed something like the meeting of a journalist with an interesting person. Nicodemus was an intellectual who, intrigued by this new religious phenomenon, made an appointment to meet with Jesus at night. He began the conversation with the traditional *captatio benevolentiae*, a goodwill gesture, praising his conversation partner. But Jesus did not allow Himself to be lured into Nicodemus's way of thinking, and in no way did He try to approach Nicodemus's expectations, prejudices, or doubts. On the contrary, Jesus immediately spoke using a mysterious, incomprehensible vocabulary. Their conversation took place on two opposing levels. Jesus was insisting on the necessity of rebirth. Today, we recognize in these words a teaching on Baptism, but Nicodemus could not guess this. His reasoning was purely natural, relating to known physiological phenomena. Thus, the thought of rebirth, understood as a return to the womb of the mother, seemed to him absurd. Jesus was not disturbed by his resistance, which on a rational level was clearly justified. He just continued his mysterious discourse. In the end, in order to break open Nicodemus's stubborn insistence on staying within the frame of a completely rational discourse and to lead him toward faith, Jesus applied a delicate means, which was to pierce through the bubble of his intellectual pride. "You are the teacher of Israel, and you do not know these things?" (John 3:10). Such a mockery of Nicodemus's self-satisfied intellectualism proved necessary so that he would believe.

A second, similar dialogue was the conversation with the Samaritan woman by the well. She was not an intellectual, but a sensual woman. She had committed adultery with many men but had never married anyone. Her immorality must have left her deeply hurt, both emotionally and spiritually. Despite this, Jesus discerned that it was possible to reveal to her the coming Paschal Mystery and to teach her about the heights of prayer in the Holy Spirit. Like the conversation with Nicodemus, their exchange initially took place on two levels. Jesus spoke to the Samaritan woman about grace and about the source of water that wells up to eternal life (John 4:14), while she thought He was speaking about the water in the well. The clash of these two conflicting discourses could lead only to a complete misunderstanding, up to the moment when Jesus brushed against the deepest poverty of this woman. When He touched her deepest wound, she immediately transferred to the level of faith and began asking about prayer. In response to Jesus' request, "Believe Me, woman" (Jn. 4:21), her heart opened and she received the healing power that was so strong that at that very moment she became an apostle of Jesus in her own city. By entrusting herself to Jesus, her justification took place. She became filled with the healing mercy of Jesus and His justice. It was not a case of treating the Samaritan woman as just, which would have meant that her sinful past was downplayed. It was a true transformation of her interiority by the power of the grace.

In justification that takes place through faith directed toward Jesus there is always the entrusting of oneself to Him. It is surrender to Him, a casting of one's human poverty onto His shoulders as

He holds the Cross, in the conviction and hope that in the risen Christ, stronger than sin and death, there is sanctifying power.

The disciples' reflection on faith

St. Paul tirelessly wrote about the justification that was, and is, accomplished as a consequence of the gift of self of Christ within the Paschal Mystery. The Cross of Christ is for us the "power of God and the wisdom of God" (1 Cor. 1:24). It is thanks to the cross that the "justice of God comes through faith to everyone … who believes in Jesus Christ" (Rom. 3:22). Salvation is accomplished by the grace of God, but the opening to it is through faith (Eph. 2:8). This is why it is through the Spirit that we eagerly await by faith the righteousness for which we hope (see Gal. 5:5). From the moment of his meeting with Christ on the road to Damascus, St. Paul was convinced that only in Him could salvation be found. Hence in his preaching and writing "there were none of the arguments that belong to philosophy," that is, arguments deriving from a rational discourse. Instead, his letters were "a demonstration of the power of the Spirit" so that the faith of those to whom he wrote would "not depend on human philosophy but on the power of God" (1 Cor. 2:4–5). This faith, in turn, is not to be a mere declaration of belief, but a living faith, "which works through love" (Gal. 5:6).

Similarly, St. Peter wrote to Christians as to a people who were "chosen" (1 Pet. 1:1–2), gifted with grace. "Through your faith," he told them, "God's power will guard you until the salvation" (1 Pet. 1:5). They received their faith from God. This faith as it passes through the trial of sufferings and difficult experiences is strengthened, becomes steadfast, and ultimately turns out to be "more precious than gold, which … bears testing by fire" (1 Pet. 1:7). Therefore, though "you did not see Him, yet you love Him; and still without seeing Him … you believe in Him" (1 Pet. 1:8).

"For this reason, gird the loins of your mind." In other words, train your mind so that it will free itself of the obstacles hindering it from setting off on the road, "be sober, putting all your hope in the grace that you will receive" (1 Pet. 1:13).

The author of the Letter to the Hebrews declared: "Now faith is the assurance of the things we hope for and proof of the realities that at present we do not see" (Heb. 11:1). Writing to Christians of Jewish descent, who knew the biblical tradition well, the inspired author enumerated a long catalogue of characters from the Old Testament, including Abel, Abraham, Moses, David, the martyrs of the Maccabean wars, and many others. All of them lived their lives "by faith," enduring migrations, sufferings, and persecution. They focused on the coming Christ, about whom they had only a nebulous notion. "These were all commended for their faith, yet they did not receive what was promised. God had planned something better for us, so that together with us they could be made perfect" (Heb. 11:39–40).

Repeatedly, biblical revelation points out the necessity of living out the divine gift, which makes the relationship with God possible. It is thanks to this special gift that "faith, hope, and love remain—but the greatest of these is love" (1 Cor. 13:13). In truth, it is such a gift that makes the human soul sensitive to the inner movements of the divine heart. By clinging to Christ in faith and hope, which becomes possible through the work of the Holy Spirit, the Christian is liberated from a sinful life and starts living according to the eternal love of God Himself. Christ teaches confidence in God the Father. The encounter with God is enabled by the three theological virtues: faith, hope, and supernatural love, which in their mature form always function together. Whoever lives animated by a living faith accepts with hope the fact that God is leading the way through unexpected paths of life. And so the believer responds to received love with love. Therefore, whenever we read in the Word of God about faith, we can safely interpret this faith as encompassing also hope and love.

A scrutiny of the gift of faith

The fact that in practical life the three theological virtues occur together does not mean that we can treat them as three interchangeable words expressing the same reality. Each one of them has its own specific meaning. Furthermore, the rhythm of their development may vary. This is why theological reflection scrutinizes them one by one. This allows for a more accurate grasp of the constitutive elements of the supernatural life. Reflection on these virtues in the light of the traditional teaching of the Church allows us to define exactly the encounter with God. It also facilitates the purification of the spiritual experience from inhibitions that are sometimes subconscious. These may appear in various parts of the psyche, blocking the development of the life of grace. Those who are concerned about the relationship with God ponder about this and try to attain some discernment in divine gifts. They try to give them a name and look into them so as to know how they function in the psyche and in practical life. It is not a matter of dissecting the gifts of God just for the satisfaction of some scientific curiosity. If this were to be the meaning of this endeavor, it would be an attempt to dominate God. This is always destructive to faith. God is mystery. He must therefore be known and loved as such, in a posture of kneeling adoration, and not in a scientific stance that reduces Him to the rank of an observed object.

The believing person, leaning out toward God, loving Him, needs some reassuring light on the road to the life-giving mystery. The conclusions of reflection on the theological virtues are based first of all on what we know due to divine revelation, not on what we can observe in phenomenological and psychological introspection, or in a sociological study. True theological insights are a necessary help in practical spiritual life. This is the purpose of theological inquiry.

Since the human mind cannot grasp everything in one gaze, the individual elements, which come together as the endowment given to the soul by God for union with Him, need to be discussed separately. This is why, as we scrutinize faith, pondering its essence, its functioning in the psyche, and how it directs us toward the Beatific Vision in Heaven and calls forth supernatural love, we must always remember that we are reflecting about a living faith, infused into the soul by grace, which ties in with hope and charity, opens us up to special gifts of the Holy Spirit, and stimulates further moral virtues. Faith is a part of the supernatural organism of grace; it is important because it is the first of the theological virtues. It is first in the sense that it has a fundamental meaning, also in the temporal sense, for it is in the practice of faith that everything begins. As St. John of the Cross taught, "faith alone ... is the only proximate and proportionate means to union with God."[2] Faith initiates the encounter with God, which is something more than just being dependent in one's existence on God the Creator.[3] Faith, therefore, is not the final end, but the point of departure, which

[2] *The Ascent of Mount Carmel* II, 9, 1, in *The Collected Works of Saint John of the Cross*, trans. Kieran Kavanaugh, OCD, and Otilio Rodriguez, OCD (Washington, DC: Institute of Carmelite Studies, 1991), p. 177.

[3] "It is true that God is ever present in the soul ... and thereby bestows and preserves its natural being by his sustaining presence. Yet he does not always communicate supernatural being to it. He communicates supernatural being only through love and grace, which not all souls possess. And those who do, do not possess them in the same degree. Some have attained higher degrees of love, others remain in lower degrees." St. John of the Cross, *The Ascent of Mount Carmel* II, 5, 4, in *Collected Works*, p. 163.

opens us up to a greater, deeper reality, leading to personal union with God. However, it is impossible to encounter God if we deny the truths revealed by Him. These truths have to be embraced and believed in faith.

As he tried to define the theological virtue of faith, St. Thomas Aquinas declared that it is a habit of the mind through which the eternal life begins in us and which urges the intellect to assent to that which is invisible.[4] Cardinal Avery Dulles suggested that this *inchoatio*, the opening of the eternal life, be translated as the "first installment" of grace given by God to believers.[5] In Aquinas's reasoning, this moment of initiating the "living through God" is fundamental in faith. It is so basic, in fact, that, without it, it is impossible to define faith.

Unfortunately, in the theology of the modern centuries this moment of ignition of the supernatural life was shelved, even though it was not denied outright. Perhaps it was considered obvious, and therefore theological reflection on faith concentrated mainly on the second part of the definition, the assent of the reason to that which is not immediately obvious. In this way reflections on faith centered mainly on the epistemological fact. How is it, it was asked, that among so many ways of cognition—between knowledge, conclusion, opinion, supposition, conjecture, and doubt—there appears also faith? Belief, even a natural belief, is a part of human experience, independent of the supernatural life, because in many situations one believes others without checking the veracity of what one accepts, either through a logical syllogism

[4] *Summa Theologiae* IIa-IIae, q. 4, art. 1: Fides est habitus mentis, qua inchoatur vita aeterna in nobis, faciens intellectum assentire non apparentibus.

[5] "… the first installment." Avery Dulles, *The Assurance of Things Hoped For: A Theology of Christian Faith* (New York: Oxford University Press, 1994), p. 257.

or personal experimentation. Of course, questioning the cognitive specificity of belief is possible. These questions have their place in philosophical speculation. But it is not this second moment that is most important in theological reflection on faith, and it is not decisive in the spiritual and moral life.

The focus on the assent by faith to that which is not obvious caused a shift in emphasis. Faith was discussed primarily in the context of the point of contact between faith and reason, thus, between revelation and the secular sciences, between theology and philosophy. It is true that a comprehensive presentation of faith must, of course, deal with such issues. But the first, truly more important moment of faith, which is the opening up to grace, must not be forgotten.

Faith ensures contact with God

The virtue of faith is infused into the soul by God Himself so that a contact between Him and the believer may take place. This happens not only in the first moment of faith, as during the reception of the sacrament of Baptism, or earlier, as in the case of an adult who asks for Baptism. Each time, when an act of faith is made, directing oneself toward Christ, there is the touch that was experienced by the woman at Capernaum who suffered from a hemorrhage. The power that comes from Jesus fills the soul in such an instance. In every moment of faith directed toward Christ, the outpouring of grace takes place, something that cannot be felt and recognized through conscious experience. The Gospel suggests that Jesus Himself experiences this effusion of grace, and this possibility of self-gift is a moment of joy for the entire Holy Trinity. Through an act of faith, even if brief, there is an immediate contact with God and an effusion of His mysterious life. Grace, like an underground, invisible stream, revives and refreshes the human soul with divine life, and this will have its ultimate fulfillment in eternity. God gives Himself to the believer as if in installments, giving more and more of Himself whenever there is, in the human soul, an entrusting of self to Him and the reception of the call of grace. The measure of the divine gift depends on the capacity of the human heart, on the quality of faith, and on the readiness to welcome its dynamic in life. The more frequent, the deeper, and the more enduring the perseverance in faith that mobilizes an individual to love, the more such an individual is internally transformed by the power of God. Though the reality of grace cannot be felt (yet it is necessary to believe in its reality) the moment of faith *can* be recognized. This is so because every act of faith is a communing with the mystery. The believer is aware of this and conscious that in a given moment there is an entrusting of self to God, a reaching out further than what human logic or a purely rational discourse might suggest. The believer may know very well that in this moment human arguments are not decisive and that in their place there is the surrender to God. This is based on the one and only motive that God exists, that He stood on the road, and that He invites us to rely on Him—on His ineffable, but nonetheless real, mystery.

The moment of faith that opens us to the supernatural life does not require any special knowledge or education. In its essence, the faith of a small child saying a simple prayer or coming up for first Holy Communion and the faith of an adult or the faith of an advanced mystic are all the same. In each case of making an act of faith, there is the union with God, the effusion of His grace, and the opening up onto His incomprehensible power. Even though the reception of grace does not bring about an experientially recognizable and immediate reaction, the believer does with time recognize that the encounter with God through faith and love, the relying upon Him, and the calling of His power do ultimately bring forth true spiritual fruits. The liberation from anxiety, the untangling from sin, the mobilization for a difficult, demanding love, the fostering within oneself and around oneself of a prayerful atmosphere, the leading of others toward the mystery of the living God—all of these are recognizable fruits that come in time with the opening of self to grace through faith. But in order for these fruits of grace to make themselves known, a living faith must be formed in the person, and as a result of practice there has to be formed a characteristic reflex of relying upon God.

This beginning of the eternal life in faith, the *inchoatio vitae aeternae* to which Aquinas drew attention, can be termed an "ignition." When one makes an act of faith, immediately the supernatural life is set in motion. It is as though an engine is fired up. For its development, the spiritual life will require a further hope that focuses on God, and a friendly encounter with Him in love. This union with God will embrace the entire ethos, that is, all of the dimensions of the moral life and all human endeavors. Faith at times will still need to be strengthened, to be purified from deformations and from views, aspirations, and habits that may extinguish it. But these are further issues that ensure a *growth* of faith. What is most important, however, is the initial moment of ignition, done by faith, as it expands the mind, so that it receives the mysterious God. This opening onto the living God through faith explains why faith is so important.

The forgetting or the insufficient exposition of the opening to grace through faith explains why it began to appear as a difficult moment to accept. This moving out beyond the perspective of the autonomous reason toward the revealed mystery will always be a challenging step for reason. In faith, reason takes on the position of a student, not that of a teacher. This requires intellectual humility. This, however, is not impossible for reason. A moment of reflection suffices to realize that often in various human situations reason is in a position in which it receives the truth from another. When it was forgotten that faith opens us up to the life of grace, and all that was seen in it was an intellectual assent to an unclear mystery, faith seemed to be some incomprehensible coercion, an obligation imposed by ecclesiastical authority upon the minds of believers in an arbitrary way. It is no surprise, then, that this generated resistance. Meanwhile, faith, above all, is a divine gift, which, together with the other two theological virtues, enables a union with God and an opening to His power. Above all, it needs to be remembered that faith is a means, a supernatural tool, which draws the believer toward God.

The genesis of faith

In the ancient Church there was a lengthy reflection on the genesis of faith and, therefore, of the entire supernatural order in the soul. Eventually, the thesis that, centuries later, came to be called Semi-Pelagianism was rejected. This heresy accepts the need for faith and grace, but it claims that the *first* moment of belief is the result of purely natural inquiry, and so through human reasoning and by one's own strength it is possible to bring oneself to the level of faith and the supernatural life. Remaining in this erroneous judgment blocks the life in God, because it concentrates the individual on the self and on personal reasoning. What then is missing is the acknowledgment of the primacy of God's working within the soul, and thus there is no profound and fascinating gratitude for the received grace of faith. At the second Synod in Orange, which took place in 529, the Church declared:

> If anyone says that mercy is divinely conferred upon us when, without God's grace, we believe, will, desire, strive, labor, pray, keep watch, endeavor, request, seek, knock, but

> does not confess that it is through the infusion and the inspiration of the Holy Spirit that we believe, will or are able to do these things, as is required; or if anyone subordinates the help of grace to humility or human obedience, and does not admit that it is the very gift of grace that makes us obedient and humble, one contradicts the apostle who says: "What have you that you did not receive?" (1 Cor. 4:7) and also "By the grace of God I am what I am" (1 Cor. 15:10).[6]

This teaching is clear. The list of verbs describing the yearning for God point to that which is already the fruit of grace. When a man believes, even if his faith is weak and sluggish, but he still has moments when he wants God; when he tries to focus on Him, even if he is not quite sure how this is done; when he sometimes prays, watches, tries, asks, searches, or knocks, though these movements sometimes seem to him to be ineffective: Such an individual has already been touched by the grace of God and has already been gifted with the supernatural life, which may then grow and develop.

Since faith is a gift of grace, given by the generosity of God, there is no need to dislocate ourselves, or others, out of the spiritual life through a transfer to an exclusively rational discourse. Instead, with gratitude, we need to believe in the existence of the supernatural spiritual life, even if that life in a particular person is very weak. That life needs then to be nourished appropriately so that the grace of faith will grow and truly enliven the entire soul from within. Faith grows when conscious acts of faith are made, because then there is deeper immersion in the torrents of

[6] Canon 6. See *The Christian Faith in the Doctrinal Documents of the Catholic Church*, ed. J. Neuner and J. Dupuis (New York: Alba House, 2001), no. 1918.

grace. When one forgets that faith, even the faith that is barely glowing in the soul, is already the fruit of grace, and one moves to the level of scientific discourse beyond faith, as though God did not exist—*sicut Deus non esset*—this certainly does not lead to a living faith. Whoever applies this erroneous understanding either to oneself or to others, instead of engaging in the development of the grace of faith that already exists in the soul, causes the continual stepping away from the order of faith. This transfer to the level of a rational discourse is sometimes done in the hope that it may lead to faith at some future moment, but in fact it keeps one outside of it.

Faith as the adaptation of the mind to the First Truth

Faith in its essential core is a supernatural reality. In faith understood strictly by itself—that is, without hope and charity—there is the adaptation of the human mind by God Himself, whereby it is made capable of receiving God as the First Truth. In hope God reveals Himself to the individual as the final, highest Good, which is worth aiming for. In supernatural love, known as *caritas*, the person is raised to a supernatural level and made capable of entering into friendship with God and with others in view of God. In faith, therefore, since it pertains to cognition, God reveals Himself as the First Truth on which everything is dependent. This adaptation of the mind is a gift of grace, and it takes place in every moment of faith, even in the faith of a little child who trusts in God and yearns for Him. This does not, however, mean that God accomplishes some new revelation in every moment when He grants the grace of faith. The revelation has already occurred, and most fully in Christ, the record of which we have in the Holy Scriptures. The contents of faith are therefore handed on to us by the Church. But the intuition that God truly exists and that we can encounter Him, because He rewards those who believe in Him, flows from grace. The filling up of this faith with further contents, which greatly enriches and strengthens faith, requires the teaching handed down by the Church. It may seem that this whole exposition about the supernatural quality of faith is somewhat stretched, since the contents of faith are given through the Word of God and transmitted by the Church anyway. However, this is not the case, because God's direct communication in faith, which adapts the human mind so that it will believe in Him, is a fundamental matter that cannot be trivialized. It is only because of the gift of faith that the Word of God and the teaching of the Church may be received. In faith there is something of the *kenosis* of God. Just as in revelation God freely diminished Himself by appearing in the written Word of God, and just as in the Incarnation the infinite Son of God accepted finite existence by being born as an infant of the Virgin Mary, so God, as the First Truth, on whom everything depends, accommodates Himself in faith to the very limited capacity of the human mind, preparing it so that it can receive the given Truth and assent to a realty that is greater than its cognitive capacity.

There are further consequences of the supernatural character of faith, which can in some way be observed even though the reality of grace cannot be experienced or investigated empirically. Sometimes it is possible to note a living faith, not only in some great saint, but also in ordinary people. These people may be of every age: small children, adults, and the elderly. One may wonder: Why do these people believe? Their faith is not the result of a convincing argument. It cannot be only the heritage of culture, because if that were the case, it would have died off long ago. And it is not the case that this faith is always obvious and easy. Amidst myriad inward doubts and outward difficulties, the believer believes. Why? Because this person has been touched by God and so continues to rely upon Him, even when everything around suggests that it would be better to throw away faith altogether. From the fact that faith is supernatural, it does not follow that it is deserved, or that it is automatic, and that it is not endangered. Faith is a gift of God, but its growth and protection from distortion require attention.

Faith is a supernatural gift. But it is also free. God acts within the human will, and in no way does this divine working limit the freedom of choice. In fact, it enhances it even more. Only God, as the Creator of the human will, can work within it as the first cause, whereby the action is human and divine at the same time. The act of faith of a person is therefore fully free, fully individual, and at the same time fully deriving from God. That is why the one who rejects faith bears the guilt of infidelity.

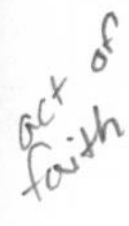

Since faith is a gift of God completely based upon God, it is always objectively certain, even though in subjective experience it is not always so. Building upon St. Augustine, St. Thomas defined an act of faith as "thinking with assent."[7] In this thinking, termed *cogitatio*, which can also be translated as "pondering"—that is, reflecting from within on that which has been received in the assent of faith—there is also space for a certain *coagitatio*—agitation. The mind of the believer ponders, penetrating the truth in which it believes, and this is accomplished through a movement of the will. But since the mind by nature tends toward light and clarity, and faith is communing with a mystery, the mind of the believer is left with a certain hunger. The believer may have an unwavering faith in God and at the same time experience great darkness. "We live by faith and not by sight" (2 Cor. 5:7). "Now we see as though through a glass, darkly" (1 Cor. 13:12). We must remember that ancient mirrors gave only a very blurry reflection. The darkness

[7] *Summa Theologiae* IIa-IIae, q. 2, art. 1: Cum assensione cogitare.

of faith is therefore normal. We should not expect that, with the passing of years, faith will necessarily become clearer. We should not likewise assume that this darkness is the consequence of sins, and that it will disappear once we have made a profound penance. Faith is the adherence of the mind to the mysterious God, Whom we cannot comprehend in full. Faith is therefore in some sense temporary, because only in eternity will it be replaced by the Beatific Vision, the seeing of God face-to-face.

Consequences

The predominance of the epistemological thread in modern theological reflection on faith and the insufficient exposition of its role in the ignition of the supernatural life were tied with a series of other shifts of emphasis in theological thought. It seems that the primacy of the theological virtues in the moral life was forgotten, and this has led to an understanding of the cultivation of the remaining virtues in a Pelagian way. In other words, there was the suggestion that, first of all, people have to correct themselves morally by their own power, and not by relying on grace, which is given precisely through the theological virtues. The excessive stress placed upon moral obligation and the narrowing of moral formation to the teaching of the Decalogue instead of the Sermon on the Mount influenced also the interpretation of faith itself, in which the obligation of belief was noted more than the fact that it is a gift of grace.

Against the background of these shifts, some further essential and important problems occurred. The intensity of the heated clashes was tied to the disappearance of awareness of the divine gift within faith. Thus, the question was posed about the possibility of salvation of those who had never heard the Gospel, as well as of infants and of those indifferent to faith. Also the issue of the relationship of nature to grace came up. When, erroneously, it was presupposed that opening toward God is the effect of natural effort, then the differentiation between nature and grace was denied. This in turn leads to the conclusion that grace is a part of nature, and so it is automatic and deserved. Meanwhile remembering that faith is a grace, a completely undeserved gift of God, leads to wondrous gratitude for the received gift that allows one to live in accord with it and grow in it, engaging in the communion of love with the self-giving God.

The recognition, therefore, of the primacy of union with God that is possible due to the gift of faith changes the believer's perspective on life. This does not, however, mean that God is denied the right to reach the human soul in multiple ways, known only to Him, eliciting the grace of faith even within a natural religiosity. But the recognition of this possibility cannot lead to the conclusion that we can give up Jesus' command to preach the Gospel and administer the sacraments, or even more that we can refrain from the conscious development of the theological virtues within ourselves, so as to base our lives ever more and ever deeply on grace.

Does this mean, then, that if we distance ourselves from faith, automatically our lives will go astray, and even slide into tragedy? After all, there are people who manage fine without faith or even without bothering about it at all, and their lives are not necessarily a wreck! But it is also true that many of those who lack the axis of faith do get lost. When the union with God is not consciously attended to, then often the result is disorientation and discouragement in the face of the difficulties of life. It is precisely at this moment that marriages and religious vocations crash. Those who have been touched by the grace of faith should not try to comfort unbelievers by telling them that without faith, they will still be happy. They also should not attempt to reach unbelievers specifically on the level of their unbelief or on the level of autonomous reason. The believer, rather, believes that faith is a divine gift that opens us to divine power. And, counting on this supernatural power, such a person simply lives out life, trusting that in others this same grace of faith will turn out to be fruitful, even if at times it seems that it has been buried.

2

Faith and Prayer

Perseverance in union with God

Faith has the capacity to trigger the movement of the supernatural life because it establishes a contact with God. Since this is the case, it is crucial that a rigorous perseverance in union with God be maintained. Common daily acts and works can be supported from within by divine grace when the intention of being attached to God is reaffirmed in faith. This desire, however, has to be aroused and renewed, because by the nature of things our attention is dissipated and in time our focus on God weakens. After all, it is impossible to concentrate continuously and solely upon God. We have to deal with life and its concerns.

The tying of oneself to God is enlivened during prayer in which faith is expressed and renewed. The growth of the supernatural life needs regular nourishment. When food is lacking, life withers and dies. Faith grows and deepens in the soul when it is exercised; it is fed by the Word of God, the sacraments, and our reactions to divine calls. When faith is not expressed or when it is expressed in only extraordinary moments, it is enfeebled. What is decisive here is not so much the public confession of faith, though, of course, that also is important, but rather its interior expression, which in the secrecy of the soul unites us with God. If somebody has no true, maintained, and cultivated interior faith and, instead, makes only public declarations of faith, these are empty. Instead of the timely confession of faith, there is only drivel. The truly believing individual carries the flame of faith within the soul, regularly renewing it through acts of faith, and in this way is united more closely to God.

Prayer as perseverance in faith

It is personal prayer that is most important for the maintenance of a lively faith. It should be as simple as possible, uncomplicated, but truly connected to God. The quality and regularity of personal prayer has an impact on communal and liturgical prayer, and on life in all its dimensions. One who cultivates personal prayer allows grace to permeate the soul. When it happens that such an individual is participating in community prayer, the true contact with God passes on also to the surroundings. When two or three people, a larger group, or even an immense crowd pray together, the contact with God established by each individual breeds a general prayerful atmosphere that disposes all those around, so that they too start expressing faith and persevering in it precisely in this moment. The common experience of grace, something that cannot be felt, but which takes place through faith that is consciously expressed and recognized in others, joins people together. As a result of this, those praying together stop being indifferent toward one another and become a community united in the common bond of faith and received grace.

The power and quality of faith that assures contact with God depend, therefore, on the quality of personal prayer that is cultivated. Whoever gives up prayer loses faith. As we try to describe prayer, we can divide it most simply among three types: vocal prayer, meditative prayer, and contemplative prayer.

In vocal prayer the praying person holds on to a given text and utters the words of a prayer or of a regular liturgical formula. The mere physical emission of the sound of the recited or sung prayer is not yet prayer. It is our faith, expressed in the moment when the words are uttered, that attributes to them the characteristics of prayer. The content of the formula of prayer that is correct—that is in accord with revealed truth—directs the mind toward the mysterious God. It has an impact on the psyche, urging the intellect and the will to ponder the proposed truth and acquiesce to it. Even more, spoken prayer focuses the entire self not only toward notions about God, but toward the living God, through the recognition of the truth about Him expressed in words. The words of the prayer, therefore, maintain the soul in its direction toward God.

During liturgical prayer, irrespective of whether one is receiving a sacrament, the psyche may be influenced by other factors. The close presence of other praying people, the beauty of the words and chants, the architecture of the church, the paintings, statues, or icons, the smell of incense—all this has an impact on the senses and disposes one to prayer. But all these artistic, emotional, or intellectual sensations in themselves are not yet prayer, even though they are conducive to it. Prayer takes place when faith is expressed in it and, even more so, when there is supernatural love of God that is based on faith. The human mind is geared toward that which is lucid, so it generally searches for clarity, but faith does not give this because it is an encounter with God, Who is mysterious. That is why perseverance in faith is sometimes difficult. But the mind has the capacity to restrain its autonomous functioning and has the ability to move beyond the level of psychic sensations and imaginations. Under the influence of the will, it may believe and persevere in faith. For this reason the use of vocal prayer, given by the trusted Church, is beneficial because it facilitates the expression of internal faith.

The next form of prayer is mental meditation. The person praying in this way generally does not seek the support of others praying simultaneously in a similar way. Instead solitude and silence are sought so as to encounter God. Such prayer may be conducted in one's own apartment, in a church, or out in the open, away from distractions. Some spiritual reading or, even better, a fragment of the Scriptures may be read calmly, even several times. The meaning of the words, which initially may have only flashed through the mind, is now grasped in greater depth. After a repeated reading of the same text, details may be perceived that initially were unnoticed, and this allows for a deeper penetration of the reading.

In the prayer of meditation, what is at stake is not just acquaintance with the text, with its literary form or historical and geographical context, with the culturally conditioned description of some event, or with the transmitted contents. Just as in vocal prayer, the exercising of the mind serves only to make the psyche more receptive, which then allows faith directed toward God to be expressed. While meditating on a scene from the Gospel, the imagination has its role, suggesting further details and prompting further development of the story. Meanwhile the mind occasionally invites the deducing of some conclusions, either of a dogmatic nature that orders thinking within faith, or of a moral nature, urging toward conversion and the introduction of some changes in one's life. During meditation one has to be watchful, so that the imagination, conclusions, conjectures, or daydreaming will not carry one far away beyond the meditated theme and beyond God, to whom the praying leads. The chosen text of the meditation can be helpful here. When the mind has drifted away, it is possible to return easily to the meditated theme.

After meditation conducted in this way, one is aware of its subject matter. If a priest intends to preach a homily about a given passage from the Gospel, meditation upon it beforehand will enlighten his mind, showing the richness of the truth contained in the text, and the priest will be able to share this with others. But the purpose of meditative prayer is not just the exercise of the mind. Meditative prayer is not the same as thinking about some issue, such as a mathematical problem. The stimulation of the mind in meditation is only a tool orienting the mind to faith, which unites the person with God.

What is most important in prayer is not mental gymnastics, nor even the drawing of conclusions, but faith that is expressed and repeated during the meditation. When the mind escapes from faith, the meditated subject matter facilitates the return to the truth of faith. But the expression of faith is something more than the cognition or the declaration of its truth or the acquisition of erudition in the field of dogmatic knowledge. In the act of faith there is the pondering with consent, the directing of the will toward God, a certain savoring of the mystery of faith that manifests something of the reality of God. We know, however, from experience that often during the prayer of meditation the mind wanders. It allows itself to be drawn to some intellectual discourse, to fictional conversations, musings, or even to the maintenance of imagined grudges and resentments. At the beginning there is a reflection on Jesus, but the perception of His goodness often quickly ends in the noting of the absence of that goodness in us. What was to be a uniting with God through faith in prayer turns out to be only an encounter with self, with brooding about the lack of some desired quality.

It is not surprising, then, that during meditative prayer, various unwanted thoughts or themes may appear. When we face God, everything that is ungodly in us comes to the surface of the psyche. But when one perseveres by returning to faith, the ungodly in us may be burned away or transformed by grace. Often during meditation, temptations, grievances, objections, and ambitions may come to the fore. The practice of meditative prayer requires attention so that one's mind holds on to only the chosen theme that is focusing one's faith. This, however, is not to be the carrying out of a self-imposed program, the forced reflection on an entire text, as if one is going through a logical syllogism or solving a mathematical problem. The purpose of meditative prayer is the exercise of faith, and so if during the meditation there is a moment when one is touched by God through faith, then this moment should be extended as far as possible. This perseverance in faith should continue, if possible, without returning to the meditation. But when the mind has drifted away to some unplanned, useless angles, the return to the chosen theme allows one to express faith anew.

The practice of contemplative prayer

The third type of prayer, contemplation, is a persistence in faith uniting us to God—not only with God the Creator, Who is upholding nature in existence, and so in some way is present in every thing, but with God, Who makes Himself available in a supernatural way. God transfigures the believer from within, enabling the believer to enter into friendship with Him and become receptive to His life and loving power. Contemplative prayer differs from meditative prayer in that the internal mental discourse is reduced to the minimum. It may appear at the beginning, but the purpose of prayer is not thinking through some issue. Prayer has the encounter with God as its end, and this takes place through faith. Even concepts about God—theological formulae of a dogmatic or moral nature that correctly grasp the truth—are put aside for a moment in this prayer, though they are not denied. This is because contemplative prayer drives deeper, beyond these concepts, to the living God Himself.[8] Theological notions, according to St. John of the Cross, are like a silver veneer, but beneath them there is gold.[9]

Faith as a product of grace rooted in the intellect and the will reaches out deeper, beyond the conceptual knowledge of God to the living God, with Whom it unites the soul. In contemplative prayer faith is exercised. The praying person initially grasps some simple truth of faith known from the Gospel or the *Catechism*, or just looks with faith at the tabernacle or an icon. There is no attempt to invent, to recall, or to plan something; there is only a simple expression of faith that God is present here, and that through faith contact is established with Him. The presence of Christ in the tabernacle cannot be understood, but, in the humility of the mind, it is possible to express an interior faith that He is here. And this perseverance in faith ensures an immediate encounter with Jesus, Who grants grace that sometimes prompts us toward love.

In the actual exercise of faith, there has to be belief in the supernatural character of faith. Faith is a gift of grace, meaning

8 "The soul is not united with God in this life through understanding, or through enjoyment, or through imagination, or through any other sense; but only faith, hope, and charity (according to the intellect, memory, and will) can unite the soul with God in this life. These virtues ... void the faculties: Faith causes darkness and a void of understanding in the intellect, hope begets an emptiness of possessions in the memory, and charity produces the nakedness and emptiness of affection and joy in all that is not God." St. John of the Cross, *The Ascent of Mount Carmel*, II, 6, 1–2, in *Collected Works*, p. 166. St. John of the Cross differs here from St. Thomas Aquinas, who located the theological virtue of hope in the will and not in the memory.

9 *Spiritual Canticle*, stanza 12, 4, in *Collected Works*, p. 516.

that it is supernatural. It does not, therefore, belong to the order of nature. It is an extra gift of God—a created but supernatural gift that is of the same nature as God, and yet at the same time is rooted in the human faculties of the mind and the will. Faith is a tool that unites with God, and we need to believe in this potency. It may seem strange, but in contemplative prayer, as faith is exercised, it is as if it is raised to a higher power. But this is so. One believes in God, and also one believes that faith is supernatural, that it has the capacity of ensuring an encounter with Him. That is why acts of faith directed toward God are repeated and then elicit supernatural love.

It is possible to persevere in such union with God. The practice of contemplative prayer, if it is regular and daily, habituates one with an encounter with God. If it happens that during this prayer the mind and imagination wander, drawing one away from the exercise of faith, it is always possible to help oneself by reading a selected text, by reciting a vocal prayer, or just by directing one's gaze toward the tabernacle or an icon. But once pure faith appears, a touching of God through faith and trust that He is here, it is possible to persevere, even for a moment, in this contact with God. Such faith, to which one can return after moments of distraction, is extremely fruitful. Since it is an exercise of faith, it expands in the soul the capacity for receiving grace. In mental prayer, the content on which one is meditating dominates, and it can even be discussed after one prays. In contemplative prayer there is no such intellectual content that could be later shared with others. There is only the encounter with God. But for the spiritual life, it has a greater fruitfulness than the mental pondering of a theme, even of a divine theological truth. In contemplative prayer it is the making of acts of faith that is the fundamental moment, because they ignite grace, setting it in motion. This faith, as the first of the theological virtues, draws with it hope, which accepts the plans that God has for us, and it elicits charity, the friendly relationship with God.

Practice is necessary for contemplative prayer, but it is not difficult. It is not the highest cognitive moment of the philosophical mind. It does not require any particular intellectual capacities.[10] It consists in making acts of faith, and that is why even children are capable of contemplative prayer. After all, for children, belief in God is easier than for adults because children are accustomed to accept many things in trustful faith. They cannot persist in concentration for a long time, but the short moments when they

[10] Contemplative prayer should not be mistaken for the act of the intellect that knows the truth directly. Some confusion has come about in theology, because in the writings of Aquinas, the Latin term *contemplatio*, which is almost synonymous with the terms *speculatio* and *meditatio*, denotes the natural functioning of the mind as it is directly cognizant of truth. *Contemplatio*, defined as a *simplex intuitus veritatis*, a direct intuition of truth, does not necessarily mean prayer. This term can easily be applied to aesthetical, mathematical, or philosophical contemplation. The two types of life, the *vita contemplativa* and *vita activa*, mentioned by Aquinas (*Summa Theologiae* IIa-IIae, qq. 180–182), refer to the academic life, which studies truth, and the active life dealing with practical affairs. Both these forms of life, like every dimension of life, may, of course, be lived out in faith. But being engaged in the cognition of truth is not necessarily prayer. If we want to find the teaching of Aquinas on the union with God, we need to study his treatises on the theological virtues and the related gifts of the Holy Spirit, and not his use of the term *contemplatio*. In fact, Aquinas notes that the person engaged in the practical life is sometimes forced by daily difficulties to refer to God in faith more so than the individual devoted to the intellectual research of truth, who may persist in self-satisfaction. And so he writes in *Super Evangelium S. Ioannis lectura*, 2640: Sed vita activa, quae signatur per Petrum plus diligit Deum quam vita contemplativa, quae significatur per Ioannem; quia magis sentit praesentis vitae angustias, et aestuantius ad eis liberari desiderat et ad Deum ire.

believe God and commend themselves to Him are true moments of contemplative prayer. In religious education children should not be required to understand everything, nor should themes that they do not understand be deleted from catechetical programs. Most of the truths that children learn about in catechesis transcend understanding. Adults also do not understand the Triune God, the Incarnation, the Redemption, and the Resurrection of Jesus, or the sacraments. Such truths can be received in faith, and, as faith is exercised, the focus upon God may be maintained and in this the soul is opened to an effusion of grace. When children trust in God and accept revealed truths that are beyond the cognitive capacities of the mind, and when they persevere in them, they are already engaged in contemplative prayer of the highest order. It is essential, therefore, that both children and adults be trained in such prayer.

The arranging of a daily schedule of life in such a way that half an hour is set aside for staying in faith with God requires some planning, but it is possible. It is irrelevant whether this time given to God be in the morning or the evening, in one's own home or in a church when there are no services there. The rhythm of daily prayer has to be adapted to one's occupation and psyche. Some people pray better in the morning, others in the evening. It is essential, however, that this special and extended time for meeting God in faith and love be maintained on a daily basis.

The practice of such prayer conducted regularly changes life deeply, because it permits the transfiguration of the human interior by divine grace. In moments of silent prayer, one expresses a childlike persistence in the face of God, awaiting His gift of grace free from paralyzing thoughts about oneself, one's sins, and one's blunders in life. What is central is God, Who is merciful and loving and Who grants His grace. A lively faith, maintained in the moment of prayer opens one to that gift. The attitude toward God is childlike, but the arranging of the day in such a way that there is time for prayer requires a certain maturity. And so faith in contemplative prayer is childlike, but it is the prayer of an adult who treats the relationship with God in a serious and responsible way. Concern about union with God through prayer that expresses faith and love for Him is much more important than the combating of moral weaknesses. That is why the encounter with God should not be transferred to some distant, impossible time, after sin is presumably overcome. First of all, the lively encounter with God has to be established and, as a result, through the power of received grace, sins will start disappearing on their own. The proximity with God is also more important than theological erudition, although this is, indeed, helpful when it nourishes faith.

The repetition of acts of faith in contemplative prayer does sometimes turn out to be difficult because various distractions flash across the psyche. What is decisive, however, is the repeated returning to God. If the psyche were to function well, like a good radio tuned once to the proper station and receiving without intermittence, there would be only one act of faith, expressed at the beginning. But often during the time that was planned for prayer, the mind is carried away in distractions or by the imagination. Each time the praying person becomes aware of the drifting away from faith, it is possible to turn to God again. Thus, during distracted prayer the love for God is repeated often. Such mangled prayer, in which there are multiple returns, is very fruitful, because the living faith is expressed several times, and it is faith that opens to grace. Furthermore, such returns to God habituate one to referring to Him in faith and in giving of oneself to Him, and this is important in daily life. There are many situations in which some good work is undertaken, sometimes something really minute, but in that moment demanding. The only reason it is done is the desire to give some pleasure to God, so that through this human generosity He will experience the joy of giving Himself.

The darkness of faith in prayer and within generosity

In the letters of St. Thérèse of Lisieux we find echoes of the difficulties that she experienced as she persisted in her attachment to God during prayer. She succeeded in combating these moments with further acts of faith and love. When she had the impression that Jesus was not answering her in prayer, she responded by telling Him that she loved him.[11] On another occasion, in a letter to her sister, she compared constancy in prayer to a sea voyage:

> A LITTLE *child all alone* on the sea, in a boat lost in the midst of the stormy waves, could she know whether she is close or far from port? While her eyes still contemplate the shore which she left, she knows how far she has gone, and, seeing the land getting farther away, she cannot contain her childish joy. Oh! she says, here I am soon at the end of my journey. But the more the shore recedes, the vaster the ocean also appears. Then the little child's KNOWLEDGE is reduced to nothing, she no longer knows where her boat is going. She does not know how to control the rudder, and the only thing she can do is to abandon herself and allow her sail to flutter in the wind.[12]

~ a voyage at sea

[11] *Letter* 110. St. Thérèse of Lisieux, *General Correspondence*, vol. I, trans. John Clarke, OCD (Washington, DC: Institute of Carmelite Studies, 1982), p. 652.

[12] *Letter* 144, St. Thérèse of Lisieux, *General Correspondence*, vol. II, trans. John Clarke, OCD (Washington, DC: Institute of Carmelite Studies, 1988), p. 803.

This surrender, *s'abandonner*, means a trustful throwing of oneself into the hands of God. Following up on this image, St. Thérèse compared the anguish of her sister with the agitation of the apostles. She urged her to trust:

> Jesus is there, *sleeping* as in the days gone by, in the boat of the fishermen of Galilee. He is sleeping ... and Céline does not *see* Him, for night has fallen on the boat.... Céline *does not hear* the voice of Jesus. The wind is blowing ... she *hears* it; she *sees* the darkness ... and Jesus *is* always *sleeping*. However, if He were to awaken only for an instant, He would have only to command the wind and the sea, and there would be great calm [Mark 4:39].[13]

Since contemplative prayer consists in the exercise of faith, it is normal that faith is dark. It is an encounter with the mystery, and so it does not give clarity. We should not expect that at some time in the future, things will be more lucid; instead we need to continue in persistence. This trustful basing of oneself upon God in the darkness can then be transposed onto daily life.

> *The wood* is not within our reach when we are in darkness, in aridities, but at least are we not obliged to throw little pieces of straw on it? Jesus is really powerful enough to keep the fire going by Himself. However, He is satisfied when He sees us put a little fuel on it. This *attentiveness* pleases Jesus, and then He throws on the fire a lot of wood. We do not see it, but we do feel the *strength* of love's warmth. I have experienced it: when I *am feeling* nothing, when I am INCAPABLE *of praying*, of practicing virtues, then is the moment for seeking opportunities, *nothings*, which please

[13] *Letter* 144, ibid., p. 804.

> Jesus more than the mastery of the world or even martyrdom suffered with generosity. For example, a smile, a friendly word, when I would want to say nothing, or put on a look of annoyance, etc., etc.[14]

In this giving of self in minute acts of love that emerge from contemplative prayer, there is the docility of the soul to the promptings of the Holy Spirit. Since faith that is exercised sets the life of grace in motion, the consequence of this is the undertaking of goodness that basically is not one's own but God's—but it works within human generosity. Toward God then, there is a trustful passivity, and toward the surroundings there is generosity, which manifests itself not so much in the quantity and magnitude of the undertaken activities, but in the quality of love that animates them.

> Merit does not consist in doing or in giving much, but rather in receiving, in loving much.... It is said, it is much sweeter to give than to receive [Acts 20:35], and it is true. But when Jesus wills to take *for Himself the sweetness of giving*, it would not be gracious to refuse. Let us allow Him to take and give all He wills. Perfection consists in doing His will, and the soul that surrenders itself totally to Him is called by Jesus Himself "His mother, His sister" and His whole family [Matt. 12:50].... How easy it is to please Jesus, to delight His Heart, one has only to love Him, without looking at one's self, without examining one's faults too much.[15]

Contemplative prayer in which, above all, one expresses faith directed toward God elicits active charity. It finds expression in various daily situations. The darkness of faith, experienced in persistent prayer, accustoms one toward generosity that is freely given, without

[14] *Letter* 143, ibid., p. 801.
[15] *Letter* 143, ibid., pp. 794–795.

thinking about self or about personal profits. What is central to prayer is the encounter with God and not pleasant sensations. We can meet with God only through faith. In prayer there is the experience of persisting in faith, because the acts of faith are conscious, but grace in itself is not experienced. If in some moment there is the sensation of being touched by God that, more often than not, invites one to undertake some concrete act of generosity, one should not hold on to the sensation itself. Further, such experiences should not be searched for. And one should not erroneously conclude that when such experiences are missing then there is no spiritual life.

St. Thérèse in her girlish teaching turned out to be a faithful disciple of St. John of the Cross. He had insisted that faith

> is an obscure habit because it brings us to believe divinely revealed truths that transcend every natural light and infinitely exceed all human understanding. As a result the excessive light of faith bestowed on a soul is darkness for it; a brighter light will eclipse and suppress a dimmer one. The sun so obscures all other lights.... Faith, moreover ... not only does it fail to produce knowledge and science, but ... it deprives and blinds people of any other knowledge by which they may judge it. Other knowledge is acquired by the light of the intellect, but not the knowledge of faith. Faith nullifies the light of the intellect: and if this light is not darkened, the knowledge of faith is lost.[16]

Faith directed toward Christ

Contemplative prayer takes place through the practice of faith, and within it we go beyond the formulae of faith toward the living

[16] *The Ascent of Mount Carmel* II, 3, 1. 4, in *Collected Works*, pp. 157–158.

God. This does not, however, mean that the truths of faith are to be dismissed for an exclusive focus on the subjective psychic engagement with the unimaginable God. Incidentally, it is not true that God is completely unimaginable. After all, God became visible through the Incarnation of His Son. The glorified humanity of Jesus Christ corresponds in part to our imagination and even to our emotions. The Word of God, which became flesh in Christ, can to a certain extent be grasped by our minds. That is why icons of Jesus are painted and sculptures are carved so that they will focus our minds, imagination, and emotions toward Him. And that is why in theology we study the revealed truths that were manifested in a supreme way in Christ. His Paschal Mystery is the key, which allows us to comprehend the ways of God. Our understanding, however, is always partial, but it does bring us closer to the mystery of faith.

Growth in faith requires, therefore, something more apart from an increase in theological knowledge. This is the point of the comment of St. John of the Cross, who encouraged reaching out to the living God. In the exercise of prayer with the persistence of faith, there always has to be a focusing of faith toward the very Person of Jesus Christ, Whom we know thanks to His Incarnation. The Holy Spirit working within the soul of the believer directs it toward Jesus Christ. To the measure that Jesus is known, we also know His Father.

Theories of mysticism that suggest the rejection of everything that is imaginable or notional, and so also the humanity of Jesus Christ, are erroneous. Such currents occasionally appear within Christianity, but most often they derive from non-Christian, Asian religious traditions. St. Teresa of Avila warned against this trap into which she herself had once fallen.[17] St. John of the Cross also

[17] *The Book of Her Life*, chap. 22, in *The Collected Works of St. Teresa of Avila*, vol. 1 (Washington, DC: Institute of Carmelite Studies,

insisted that Christ should not be forgotten, and no new revelations beyond what has been given in Him are to be sought.[18] Also, today, the Church warns against such deformations of mysticism.[19] The complete rejection of the content of faith associated with the practice of some notionless meditation, as in Buddhism, may lead to the search for refined, sublime, but natural psychic experiences—that is, to a concentration on self and egoism, not on the life of grace that provokes demanding expressions of love for God and love for neighbor in view of God.

Faith in liturgical prayer

When contemplative prayer, with its persistence in faith and charity focused on God, is practiced regularly, this has an impact on liturgical prayer. It is not so that each of the ways of prayer described above replaces the previous. One may regularly exercise silent faith before God and also return from time to time to the prayer of meditation, in particular when it turns out that silent prayer stops being an encounter with God and becomes only indulging in daydreaming. Also vocal prayer, especially liturgical prayer, has to be practiced throughout one's life. Habituation in silent prayer, in

---

1987), pp. 191–200. Cf. ibid., chap. 22, 8: "The most sacred humanity of Christ must not be counted in a balance with other corporeal things."

[18] "Fasten your eyes on Him alone because in Him I have spoken and revealed all and in Him you will discover even more than you ask for and desire." *The Ascent of Mount Carmel* II, 22, 5, in *Collected Works*, pp. 230–231.

[19] See Congregation for the Doctrine of the Faith, *Letter to the Bishops of the Catholic Church on Some Aspects of Christian Meditation* (October 15, 1989), http://www.vatican.va/roman_curia/congregations/cfaith/documents/rc_con_cfaith_doc_19891015_meditazione-cristiana_en.html.

which faith touching God is dominant, influences liturgical prayer and shows the spirit in which it should be celebrated.

Since, through faith, contact with God is established that triggers the effusion of grace, it follows that, when this happens in communal prayer, grace touches the entire community. But it is essential that the direction of faith toward God truly takes place during the liturgy. This has to happen not only in the soul of the main celebrant, but in all who are participating. During communal prayer, all should exercise their faith. So, too, the readers and cantors should draw attention not to themselves but to God. Also, the altar servers, the organist, those who take up the Sunday collection, and all the faithful should pray in faith. Sometimes there are liturgies in which it seems as if the altar servers are not praying, the organist is singing without faith, the priest is going through the routine motions in a mechanical way, carelessly, as if informing everybody that he is bored, and the preacher is delivering empty verbiage with no faith. In these difficult moments faith needs to be repeatedly exercised. Faith is an encounter with the mystery. And when the liturgy is celebrated in a sloppy manner, a strong, persistent faith is needed with the conviction that faith ensures a contact with God and initiates the effusion of grace.

Since faith sets grace in motion, all people, priests or laypersons, who perform acts of faith generate a prayerful climate that in time draws others to the spirit of prayer. This is sometimes very difficult for the celebrant, requiring conscious internal recollection, in particular when those present at the liturgy are not praying, but rather treating it as some social gathering. This is not so much a problem during daily Masses, because those who attend them normally truly pray. But during weddings, First Holy Communions, or funerals, often there are people in the church who are not praying at all, being interested only in the social event and in the taking of pictures. Great care is needed to ensure that there will be persistence in faith during the liturgy and that those who have found themselves occasionally in church will be drawn by the faith of others. Some technical details are useful, such as the maintenance of silence in the sacristy before proceeding to the altar and the closing of the door leading to the sacristy, in particular when there are conversations there during the celebration.

All liturgies, including those at the occasion of weddings, First Holy Communions, or ordinations, should be celebrated in such a way that they will enflame and not extinguish the spirit of prayer. In the past, pictures and, even more so, videos were not taken in such moments. If there were pictures, they were shot after the celebration and outside the church. When the first place in the liturgical celebration is attributed to the photographer, this wipes out the spirit of prayer. In churches that are visited by tourists because of their works of art, ways must be found to ensure that there will be silence in them, that mobile phones are turned off, and that at least a part of the church is reserved for those who come to pray.[20]

Persistence in faith during prayer is not a question of emotions. One does not have to have a sad face or be indifferent toward others. Prayer does not consist in emotional rigidity. Prayer is the practice of faith, the humility of the mind that reaches out toward the mystery, and not the activation of the emotions.

Concern for prayerfulness during the liturgy does not necessarily mean that old liturgical vestments, which were fashionable in the nineteenth century, have to be brought back. But the arrangement, decoration, and art in the church has to be such that it is conducive

[20] Italian churches and even St. Peter's Basilica in the Vatican are not examples to be imitated. The Italian church will be renewed only when the priests, bishops, religious, and faithful are convinced that great effort needs to be put into concern for the quality of faith in prayer, that a prayerful atmosphere has to be generated and not destroyed through misbehavior and rowdy chatter.

to prayer and directs the attention of the faithful toward God and not toward the celebrant or other participants of the liturgy. In Poland things are not as bad in this respect as in other local churches, where sometimes the traditional high altar with the tabernacle has been replaced by a podium, sometimes adorned with a grand piano. In some such settings the celebrant and the altar servers feel that they are like fashion models appearing in a show. It is not surprising that the positioning of the altar in such a way that it draws the attention toward the celebrant, the assistants, and the community has led to the emptying of churches. This does not mean, however, that everything in Poland is ideal. The temptation to mechanical celebrations, particularly in churches that have several Masses during the day and in which the organist is singing the same chants and the priest is repeating the same homily, or in large urban cemeteries where the chaplain has a funeral every fifteen minutes, is a real danger. Care has to be taken to ensure that liturgical prayer is truly a moment in which faith and love are directed toward God. Each priest and each layperson may influence the prayerful atmosphere during liturgical gatherings. Faith that is truly expressed in the soul unites one to God and draws divine grace.

A special moment for the awakening or renewal of grace, including the grace of faith, is the reception of the sacraments. They are not just occasions to remind oneself about God, Who gives Himself to us anyway. In the sacraments there is a new, objective meeting with God, Who gives Himself through the physical sign of the sacrament. The force of the sacraments derives from the gift of self made by Jesus Christ, Who offered Himself on the Cross. The Son of God, Who had assumed a human physical body and conquered sin and death by the power of His charity, continues to give Himself in the Church through the sacraments.[21]

[21] *Summa Theologiae*, IIIa, q. 62, art. 5.

Always during the reception of the sacraments there is an objective meeting with God, irrespective of the power of faith of the one who administers or receives the sacrament. The priest who is celebrating Mass may be distracted; the confessor may be somewhat deaf; they even may be seriously entangled in sin: But this does not impair the validity of the sacraments. A sinful priest administers the sacraments validly and contributes through his ministry to the sanctity of the faithful. The one receiving sacraments may have a weak faith, but this does not affect their validity. We do not know what sort of faith an infant has as he or she is baptized, or the depth of faith of the family who is present. A bride may be worried about her wedding dress, thrilled about the event, and not at all prayerful, or the groom may be thinking about the fun he will have at the wild reception after the ceremony, but this does not affect or weaken the validity of the sacrament of matrimony.

Forgetting about the real, objective causality in the sacraments, something against which Aquinas vigorously warned,[22] leads to centering attention on the catechetical, social, or artistic aspects of the sacramental celebration. These dimensions may quickly wane or become boring. What is most important in the sacraments is the gift of God, given truly and anew through the sacrament, irrespective of the quality of the accompanying preaching or the prayerfulness of those present. But certainly the reception of the sacraments within a lively faith and the renewal of their graces by repeated acts of faith enhance their fruitfulness. At the wedding ceremony or during the ordination to the priesthood the receiver of the sacrament may have had a weak, distracted faith. But the living out of the graces of the sacrament and their renewal through prayer and the reception of the sacraments of Penance and the

[22] *Summa Theologiae*, IIIa, q. 62, art. 1.

Eucharist result in growth in the vocation and in the reception of graces that give the strength to persevere in it.

What is the relationship between the reception of the sacraments and the expression of faith during prayer that, after all, also unites one with God and opens one to His grace? The internally expressed faith sets the supernatural life in motion. The renewal of acts of faith animated by charity deepens the encounter with God and habituates one to a further receptivity to the power of God in the events of daily life. All this takes place in a supernatural way within the human interior, and so the power of God is not felt. Subjectively one may only recognize that the act of faith was made and that further acts were made on the basis of that trusting belief.

Meanwhile the sacraments, due to their physical, visible structure are an objective fact that is perceptible also to others and to the community of the Church. The subjective consciousness of faith may vacillate, but the objective reception of a sacrament grants certitude. During an ardent personal prayer, subjectively, somebody may be convinced that sins have been pardoned by God. But the reception of the sacrament of Penance grants the certitude that these sins have been burned away by God, and so those sins can be forgotten and life may commence anew, strengthened by grace that inclines toward goodness. Similarly, the one who for some reason cannot receive Holy Communion may, through faith that is animated by charity, receive a spiritual Communion and in this way unite with God. The objective reception of the Eucharist, however, gives the certitude that Christ has been welcomed in the heart. Similarly, the reception of sacraments that change the status of the person and generate obligations, such as Baptism, Matrimony, or Holy Orders, is objective and clear. The reception of these sacraments leaves no doubt about the status of the person and guarantees that God will not be stingy in offering the graces needed for living out one's vocation on the condition that sensitivity to these graces will be animated by a lively faith exercised in prayer.

The sacraments are therefore extremely important for the life of faith and life in the Church. But they do not dispense one from the necessity of caring for one's faith and deepening it through authentic prayer that expresses faith and the love of God.

Faith and religiosity

Christian faith differs from religiosity because faith is a particular gift of God. That is why it is inappropriate to speak about Islamic faith or, even more so, about Buddhist faith. But we can speak about religiosity beyond Christianity. This is because religiosity belongs to the natural moral order. It is a virtue allied with justice that expresses rendering due worship to God. Religiosity derives from the natural desire for the vision of God, which is an extension of cognitive curiosity.

Since, through natural reason, we can perceive that the existing reality is dependent on some Absolute, so also can we arrive at the conclusion that a recognition of this Absolute is owed. In every religiosity there is some recognized cognitive content, some cult of the Supreme Being and some moral conclusions deriving from the order which has its ultimate foundation in the Absolute. Religiosity is the consequence of the most sublime natural desire that is in man. Being a religious person is therefore a sign of great humanism. Humans reach out in various ways toward the Absolute. There are traces of religiosity found in all continents and historical periods. This is seen in the wide variety of funeral customs. When an animal dies, the carcass is devoured by other animals. When a human being dies, the corpse is buried or cremated in a way that manifests respect for the person and the individual's mystery. Since religiosity is manifested in some rites, practices, and ethical rules, its manifestations may be the subject of scientific observation in the fields of sociology, cultural anthropology, and also psychology and history.

Religiosity imposes an axis and order upon all other natural human desires. Religiosity is not only individual but also social, and so it brings equilibrium to societies. Those societies that have arrived at a state of no religion are tottering, lacking certitude about social mores, and succumbing to ideological and political manipulations. And, finally, they find themselves worshipping some new, sometimes bizarre religion. Meanwhile societies that have a strong religious tradition are rooted in it. The main focus of religiosity, however, is from below to above, that is, from man toward the Absolute. Meanwhile, in faith, the focus is from above to below; divine grace is showered upon people.

What, therefore, is the relationship between faith and religiosity? The thesis that claims that since religiosity derives from nature it is some form of idolatry, which must be contrasted with pure faith deriving from God, is unjustified. This basically Protestant view suggests that grace does not fit human nature, which has no capacity for the reception of the gift of faith. Faith is said to be a purely external, supernatural gift. This thesis introduces an unhealthy chasm between grace and nature, and so between the spiritual and the religious life, which has a visible, social dimension.

In reality, faith, even though it is a supernatural gift that opens one to divine grace, is rooted in the human faculties and elicits real attitudes, including social ones, and generates true prayer. Faith, therefore, changes religiosity from within, attributing to it a supernatural fecundity. In turn, religiosity supplies faith with a protective structure that allows for its social expression. Where faith is alive, renewed by true prayer consciously directed toward God and animated by charity, its influence becomes visible in expressions of religiosity, and these in turn nourish and sustain the faith—both of those who participate in religious rites with a deep faith and of those who happen to be present in some service and are drawn into the lively faith of others. But when a living faith is lacking in religious services, or when these services are empty—celebrated in a routine way, or uniquely for social or political reasons—they do not nourish faith and, even more, they become repulsive. A true believer feels uneasy in such manifestations of empty religiosity, sensing some manipulation of holy things for other unholy ends. True faith, even though it is delicate and seemingly elusive, has its power. Whoever has tasted the encounter with God does not want to give it up, nor does he want to participate in services that are off-putting by their superficiality and mechanical routine, like political meetings, concerts, or social gatherings rather than true liturgies.

The Church is always faced with the challenge of purifying existing forms of religiosity. The sacramental liturgy, of course, is not the private property of the priest; it is subject to ecclesial authority. Many other services and religious customs are not under such precise scrutiny of the pastors. Their differentiation, depending on historical periods and countries, points to the social grassroots input in the formation, maintenance, and renewal of popular religious customs. It is not surprising that religious customs deriving from distant countries, for example, from southern Italy or Latin America, may not touch hearts in the same way as native traditions. But also local customs may at times arrive at the stage of exhaustion. Weariness with them does not necessarily have to signify an immediate absence of faith or the lack of a desire to deepen it. Fatigue with certain forms of piety, particularly if they are celebrated in a routine way, may be simultaneously tied with an authentic yearning for a life of faith and a desperate search for ways of deepening it.

What is most important is the interior attitude in which the living faith is exercised, and this has to be the main focus of concern.

However, it is also necessary to reflect occasionally upon the inherited forms of religiosity. For example, do they belong to rural traditions that do not correspond to urban life? Are they tied with an imprecise theology, more akin to folk Christmas carols than to revelation, the theology of the saints, and the Magisterium of the Church, and so need to be renewed? And are some new forms of religiosity too banal, dependent upon quickly passing fashions? Are new church architecture and art truly sacred and conducive to faith, or were they generated outside of faith, or even inspired by ideas contrary to a true theology that nourishes faith?

3

Is It Essential That the Confessed Faith Be Exact?

Imprecision in the confessed faith

Auguste Sabatier, a nineteenth-century French Protestant theologian, claimed that justification through faith liberates the Christian from the bondage of dogmas, creeds, bishops, and priests. He rejected the external rule of faith supplied by ecclesiastical authority and recognized only the internal subjective experience of faith that entails a movement of the Holy Spirit but does not need any focusing.[23] This view is repeated often, sometimes through the phrase "Deeds, not creeds!" It suggests that precision in the formulations of faith is immaterial. What supposedly is uniquely important are personal religious experiences and activity generated by them. Thus, faith is said to consist only in trust in God, whereas the intellectual assent to a specific revealed content is purely optional and irrelevant. Earlier John Calvin made the accusation that Catholics recognize that faith has certain binding subject matter,

[23] Dulles, *The Assurance of Things Hoped For*, p. 97.

but they leave its formulation to the Church hierarchy, and then they brag about their theological ignorance.[24]

Is it essential that the confessed faith be known and correctly expressed? And how are we to assess believers who are searching for God, loving Him, and taking Him into account in their daily lives, but who, when it comes to the articulation of their faith, commit evident errors because their catechetical knowledge is quite poor relative to their knowledge and stature in other fields? Is it possible that true, salvific faith deriving from God could be located among erroneous, but firmly held, theological opinions, folk customs, and religious songs that contain dogmatically false expressions? The Church recognizes the authenticity and value of the faith of non-Catholic Christians while She firmly rejects some of their dogmatic and moral statements. Does this mean that the subject matter of the confessed faith is inessential for its liveliness and capacity of stimulating grace in the soul? Is it possible that within the attitude of an irate adolescent who rejects religious practices or that of an adult who directly declares his lack of faith, there might still be a true, supernatural faith that makes contact God and His grace? Or maybe the richness of the content of faith is greater than what can be verbally expressed, just as knowledge is more extensive than what can be precisely articulated? The subject matter of faith is conveyed not only by exact creedal formulas, dogmatic statements, and published catechisms. It is also carried by the rich and various ways of expressing and deepening it—above all through the liturgy, but also through various religious traditions, devotions, poetry, moral convictions, and schools of spirituality, not all of which are characterized by precision in their formulations.

We cannot accept the thesis that the subject matter of the confessed faith is irrelevant so long as there is trust in God. This

[24] Ibid., p. 48.

is because serious errors on the theoretical level generate erroneous consequences on the level of practical life. When somebody accepts intellectually the Manichaean principle that there are two equally powerful gods, one of whom is good and the other evil, and that the choice between them is purely arbitrary, then such an individual is on a false track leading to moral catastrophe. If somebody treats the world as god, rejecting the distinction between the Creator and the creature, this then entails a deification of that which is temporal, in which the individual is entrapped. Those who believe in reincarnation do not appreciate the uniqueness of their life and therefore do not treat it with due seriousness. Those who reject the truth about the Blessed Trinity do not perceive the paternity of God and His mercy and therefore fall into a dependency on a divinely imposed fate. If somebody denies the free intervention of God in revelation and reduces religiosity to the level of a socially useful custom, then basically that religiosity is deemed to be meaningless. Dogmatic errors deform human life in a deeper and more fundamental way than moral errors. The precise cognition of the truths of faith is critical and must not be scorned.

Faith undoubtedly is a gift of grace given generously by God, as a result of which the intellect and the will are focused toward God and the metaphysical chasm between humans and God—between nature and grace—is transcended. When acts of faith are exercised, there is a union of the believer with God and the soul is opened toward the torrents of His grace. It is not an irrelevant issue whether it is considered that this is an encounter with the living God and not with some sort of inexpressible Buddhist void or whether it is only the reception of a conclusion of pure intellectual curiosity. "Anyone who comes to Him [God] must believe," at least, "that He exists and rewards those who try to find Him" (Heb. 11:6). It is much better when the believer not only recognizes in some nebulous way that God responds to human cries, but also consciously believes that this is done through the Son of God Who, being incarnate, has redeemed us, freeing us from sin and granting us His own life through the Holy Spirit.

The content of faith

A conscious faith is focused on Christ, and so it includes specific truths about the Triune God, about the history of salvation, about the Incarnation and the Redemption, about the Church and Her sacraments, and about moral principles given by Jesus that show how it is possible to live by grace. The gift of grace that enables faith—through which God as the First Truth overpowers the human intellect, and partly also the human will, and leads to hope and the supernatural love of charity—is fundamental and primary. This gift, however, does not immediately contain all the truths of faith. God does not grant His revelation to individuals. The subject matter of faith has been transmitted once and for all in the public revelation, which ended with the death of the last apostle. What has been revealed is constantly announced, known in depth, and faithfully handed down by the Church. The reception therefore of the truths of faith has to be such as they are expressed by the Church.

The subject matter of faith is important because it focuses the mind correctly toward Christ, in Whom there is salvation. It also shows how to live in accord with His gift. The gift of the grace of faith makes the intellect and the will ready to receive God, but the more precise content of this faith that speaks of God and His actions toward us has to be received from the hands of the Church. The Church transmits this, not as Her arbitrary invention, but as coming from the revealed Word of God.

Just as, in the Incarnation, the Son of God, the eternal Word of the Father, has appeared in the form of an infant, so, in faith, God, the First Truth, goes through a sort of kenotic diminution, becoming the object of the human mind. The infinite God is somehow adapted in this to the limited capacity of the human mind. The question therefore can be raised: Can the content of faith, as it is grasped with the help of human concepts and then transmitted, really and truly encompass God? Are the words, the terms, and the expressed formulations of faith only a human approximation of the divine contents, which may later, depending on the perceived needs and current prejudices, be freely replaced by other concepts that are more approachable and meaningful? Or do these enunciations truly home in on God Himself and so, when they are passed on or translated from one language to another, must reflect precisely the reality they contain?

Medieval theology raised the question of whether the mind of the believer grasps the very reality of God—that is, the *res*—or whether it grasps only the concepts or words that can be said about God—that is, the *enuntiabilia*. Does faith arrive at the simple, indivisible reality of God, or does it stop short at the level of diverse human formulations that are conditioned culturally and historically? The response to this question was tied to the reading of the history of salvation. Was the faith of the Jews before the coming of Jesus the same as the faith of Christians after His coming? The Jews believed in the future Messiah, and Christians believe in Christ, Who has already come, Who died on the Cross, and Who was raised from the dead. Is the object of faith identical in both cases? In other words, does the faith of the believer terminate only in the acquisition of concepts of God that have their historical and cultural limitations, and were described as silver surfaces of the image of St. John of the Cross? Or does faith reach out to the reality itself, to God, that is, to the gold that is beneath the silver surface? Faith, as the Church teaches, is a gift of grace infused in the soul by God; thus it would be strange if that faith did not have the capacity of reaching God directly and instead stopped short, at only the level of bare concepts. But the question about the function of these concepts remains. The answer given impacts the understanding of the role of formulas that grasp the content of faith.

Aquinas rejected a strict either-or understanding of our ability to grasp God—that is, that what we can grasp is either the *res*—namely, reality itself—or merely the *enuntiabilia*—that is, the enunciations of faith. Rather, he argued that faith grasps the reality itself, toward which it is ordered, but this takes place *through* the enunciations. The words of faith are not just some sort of screen or shadow of reality. They are a means that serve the union with the reality of God. The object of faith that is God will be grasped in Heaven in Himself in His infinite simplicity, whereas here on earth He may be grasped by the mind only through composite concepts. These are subject to a necessary psychic conditioning so that the mind will adhere to God. This distinction is not outlandish or bizarre. Something similar takes place also in the cognition of other sciences. In grammar and logic the mind abstracts from reality and deals only with predication and reasoning, whereas in other sciences, just as in faith, the mind reaches through expressions to the reality itself that it grasps. In Heaven we will reach out to God in the simple grasping of the intellect, but so long as we are on earth, we have to approach Him in faith with the help of concepts. These concepts, therefore, are not a hindrance, because they extend beyond their verbal contents and lead to the living God.[25]

This strange medieval debate about the object of faith points to the human characteristics of the psychology of the act of faith. Faith is a supernatural reality. It is a gift of grace, but this gift takes place within the human psyche. This means, therefore, that it is

[25] *Summa Theologiae*, IIa-IIae, q. 1, art. 2, ad. 2: Actus autem credentis non terminatur ad enuntiabile, sed ad rem.

subjected to a certain kenotic diminution, and so it is open to all the weaknesses and limitations of human conditioning.

Since the simple and pure reality of God, the First Truth, accedes to the mind through concepts, conclusions, and predications, might not these human concepts influence decisively, and maybe even arbitrarily, the truths of faith? Faith can speak about God thanks to revelation, which proceeded in history, availing itself of concepts that were the product of culture. These concepts, taken from life and human experience, have been handed down to us especially through the Hebrew and Greek languages. Words such as "father," "shepherd," and "teacher" employed by revelation are comprehensible in their natural sense. Even those who do not believe in God can understand their natural meaning. But ever since God used these human concepts, they acquired in revelation a new and deeper meaning. The word "father" has existed for centuries in human societies, but in revelation it acquired a new depth—and natural human paternity is only a shadow of it. Also, words that revelation has not employed, but the Church uses, such as "Trinity" and "sacrament," also have their natural sense, which is subjected to transformation within faith. Similarly, the word "person," which in Greek referred to the mask used by an actor in the theater, acquired a new meaning in the language of faith, when it was applied to a divine Person, and then to a human person.

In using human expressions, faith reaches out to supernatural reality, which has not been worked out by an arbitrary human invention, but has been given by God. The reception of the contents of faith by the mind urges it to incline in the face of a reality that transcends it and forms it. Biblical theology, with the help of precise methods, reaches out to ancient literature, to linguistics, and to the results of archaeological excavations so as to understand exactly the natural meaning of the terms that were used by the authors of the Bible. Then, through the analogy of faith, searching for the connections between the mysteries of faith and relating them to Christ, the Word of the Father, it probes deeper to their spiritual meaning, to the divine reality expressed through these human concepts. Finally, speculative theology tries to articulate the spiritual reality with the help of simple but precise definitions and specify the meaning of its contents.

The deposit of faith in the hands of the Church

The Church has received the deposit of faith from God and with the assistance of the Holy Spirit tries to penetrate its contents. But the Church did not receive the right to rework this deposit in arbitrary fashion. We cannot say that in history there was a distinct revelation for the Jews, another revelation for the Greeks, and another for the Slavs. The truths of faith were handed down once and for all and the Holy Scriptures have reached us through the Hebrew and Greek languages. As each nation receives the deposit of faith, it brings into its religious sensibility its own cultural input, of course, but the Church must take care that this input does not deform the content of faith derived from revelation. This has been particularly important since the Second Vatican Council, which permitted the use of vernacular languages in the liturgy of the Latin Church. The Church must ensure that the translation of liturgical texts into Vietnamese, Finnish, or Tagalog be faithful, and that certain local traditions—such as the Polish palms on Palm Sunday, painted Easter eggs, or the traditions of other nations—do not distort the truths of faith about which these traditions remind us. The Church also has to react when Christian tradition is deformed and elements totally foreign to faith are glued onto it, as has happened with the vigil of the solemnity of All Saints (All Hallows) being transformed into Halloween, and as happens when Christmas is reworked into a shopping spree.

It cannot be held that expressions of the faith may differ in the essentials. This would mean that some truths of faith would be binding in Ukraine and others in Uganda. The enunciations of faith as they are translated from one language to another have to be exact, in accord with the deposit received in revelation. The same is also true when in a given culture some changes in the meaning of concepts have appeared, thereby generating resistances, and so further elucidations and reformulations of the truths of the faith are needed. What is at stake is that the enunciations of faith do not elicit erroneous perceptions, because their purpose is the faithful focusing of the mind toward God, the First Truth. It cannot be that each culture works out its "own truth of faith" on the basis of its cultural heritage, which may differ from the deposit of faith that the Church has received. Such a "private truth" would cease to be true. The Church cannot permit this because even the Church does not adhere *directly* to the entire contents of the divine truth, which the Church would then have to express in a human language. Rather, the Church has received the expression of this truth already in a human way, given at a specific time through the biblical languages and their culture. The Word of God has been disclosed on the pages of the Holy Scriptures, and it has been revealed in its plenitude as incarnate in the humanity of Jesus Christ. As we ponder on the truths of faith and penetrate their profound meaning, we need constantly to return to the Holy Scriptures, but we need also to remember that the fullness of revelation is not in the written text itself, but in Christ. Thus, only union with the living, risen Lord in faith allows for an appropriate reading of the Scriptures.

In the Gospels we find many terms that describe Jesus. He is called a "rabbi," a "gate," a "good shepherd," "the way, the truth and life." The most important designations declare that He is the Son of the heavenly Father and the Word that became flesh.

Following St. Augustine, St. Thomas Aquinas undertook an in-depth reflection on the meaning of the term "Word," *Logos*. He concluded that, just as in the process of thinking, various conjectures and opinions are set together until the moment comes when a final concept appears in the mind, grasping the truth in its basic contours, so also in the Word that became flesh we need to recognize the divine concept, the divine notion, the idea of God for us humans that has been given to us most fully in Christ.[26] This divine concept, manifested in the incarnate *Logos*, in Christ is binding for the Church. It offers a basic orientation, even if as a result the Church finds herself in opposition to the world. Jesus was aware of this, and He expressed it in His prayer to the Father as He summarized His mission: "I passed Your word on to them, and the world hated them, because they do not belong to the world, no more than I belong to the world" (John 17:14).

It is only in the reception, through faith, of Jesus, together with His Paschal Mystery, in which the eternal project of the heavenly Father that is His mysterious plan for the world was disclosed (see Eph. 3:3–11), that an appropriate reading of the Holy Scriptures and an interpretation of one's own life and plans is possible. The disciples on the way to Emmaus learned about this when Jesus explained to them how to read the Holy Scriptures and how to allow the divine mystery to penetrate their hopes and expectations (Luke 24:26–27).

Those who want to know the Word of God in its purest form, meaning the divine project for us, need above all to direct their faith to Christ, the Word of the Father, and then they need to read the Holy Scriptures, preferably in the original—that is, in

[26] *Summa Theologiae*, Ia, q. 34, art. 2; q. 107, art. 1; Ia-IIae, q. 93, art. 1, ad. 2; cf. H. Paissac, *Théologie du Verbe: Saint Augustin et saint Thomas* (Paris: Cerf, 1951).

the Hebrew or Greek version—interpreting them through the Paschal Mystery.[27] The Old Testament has to be read in the light of the New, taking into account the Paschal Mystery, and not in reverse fashion, because this would lock the divine gift within the Jewish tradition. The declarations of faith that progressed during the history of the Church—even though they were triggered by various newly raised questions and the internal life of faith of the Church, as a result of which the truth was expressed through numerous languages and concepts—always had the purpose of transmitting the same Word of God, the same deposit of faith, "in the same teaching, in the same meaning, and in the same opinion," as St. Vincent of Lerins expressed it.[28] Faith is indeed a gift of grace, but since its subject matter is handed down, there is a danger of error in this transmission. The believer is not infallible in the expression of faith merely by reason of the fact that the grace of faith has been received from God. Every individual has to acquire knowledge of the contents of faith as it is received from the Church. This requires some intellectual effort and the occasional checking of whether what one has received is truly the teaching passed on by the Church—or maybe it is only somebody's private opinion. If this effort and fidelity toward the received deposit are missing, errors may slip in.

[27] Incidentally, the primacy of Jesus, the incarnate Word, above the written text of the Scriptures allows us to study it with a critical mind. In Islam, this is impossible, because the Muslims claim that the word of God became the Quran and so it is untouchable. It cannot be translated or subjected to a historical-critical reading.

[28] *Commonitorium*, no. 2 (*PL* 50, 640): *quod ubique, quod semper, quod ab omnibus creditum est.* No. 23 (*PL* 50, 668): *In eodem scilicet dogmata, eodem sensu eademque sententia. The Faith of the Early Fathers*, vol. III, trans. W. A. Jurgens (Collegeville, MN: Liturgical Press, 1979), p. 265.

Only the Church possesses the charism of infallibility, and this is only when dogmas of the faith are announced officially. In the everyday teaching of the faith, the Church has the assistance of the Holy Spirit, in particular when it is called upon through faith by pastors and teachers. But since teaching always takes place within a cultural context, and often in response to questions that, in a given moment, seem pertinent but often narrow down the perspective, some inaccuracies, shifts of emphasis, or misunderstandings in the reception of the content of faith happen. Similarly, in religious traditions as well as in theological research, exactitude is sometimes lacking. This does not mean that within such a human environment true faith that unites with God cannot appear. Even amongst those with very poor religious knowledge and erroneous opinions, there may persist a true faith opening toward grace. Christians, who for decades lived in Siberia and were deprived of the sacraments, pastors, religious literature, and catechisms, were not automatically deprived of divine grace. But their faith was greatly endangered. It could become distorted or even extinguished.

The reception of the content of faith

Serious errors come about most often when the revealing God is not recognized as the appropriate motive of faith and instead some other motives are put in place. When statements concerning the faith are accepted specifically because they are the view of scientists, historians, archaeologists, astronomers, or psychologists, or only because they correspond to fashionable ideologies or political plans that then become more important than the Word of God, then an error that deforms faith will certainly appear. Faith in the Resurrection of Jesus is based not on the results of scientific studies made on the Shroud of Turin, but on God Himself. There needs to be concern for the purity of the motive of faith. St. Thomas the apostle believed in the risen Lord, not because he was convinced by his empirical observation of Jesus' body (John 20:24–29). With his physical eyes he saw the man Jesus with wounds on His body, as a result of which he had some natural knowledge about that body, but with the eyes of faith he believed in Christ the Savior.[29] The faith of the apostle reached out further than just noting an inexplicable phenomenon that seemed miraculous and to which the reason could relate. The faith of St. Thomas adhered to the mystery of Christ, the Lord and God, that is, to the supernatural reality that was the object of his faith.

It happens sometimes that true faith is intermingled in the minds of people with opinions or scientific theses that seem to be contrary to faith. This is problematic. But it also happens that true faith is intermingled with opinions or scientific theses that appear to be in accord with faith, and this may also cut faith down if it is based on these opinions or scientific theses and not on the simple motive that God has in fact spoken, thus disclosing Himself. In such a case, what is missing is the discernment and capacity of sifting out that which really belongs to faith from views, scientific statements, political programs, or myths that are external to it.

The concord of faith and knowledge may be a difficult cross for the mind, sometimes leading to a simplistic conclusion based solely on natural argumentation, thereby closing the door to the mystery. Faith is not to be reduced to the level of a purely rational conclusion in which it is justified by arguments deriving from scientific knowledge, because this stretches the capabilities of either faith or knowledge. Similarly, the simultaneous fideistic recognition of faith and a thesis that is directly contrary to it cannot be allowed.

[29] Quoting St. Gregory the Great, St. Thomas Aquinas wrote about St. Thomas the apostle: *Aliud vidit et aliud credit. Summa Theologiae*, IIa-IIae, q. 1, art. 4, ad. 1.

For example: "On the one hand, I believe in the reality of the Eucharist, and, on the other hand, I regard it as being impossible." The human mind does sometimes fall into such contradictions, and in history there were cases of the intermingling and mistaking of scientific views with faith. It is important, therefore, that faith will be purified both in the sense of separating it from views, errors, and secondary motives that accompany it, and in the sense of its deeper rooting in the mind in such a way that it influences thinking and decision-making.

Faith, as a gift of grace infused in the soul that opens us to divine life, and the basic content of faith transmitted by the Church as a deposit of faith that leads to God are not based on independently reasoned arguments or philosophical or scientific conclusions, or even on the authority of the Church; instead, they are based on the authority of the self-disclosing God, Who cannot err. In faith, God embraces the human mind, leading it to Himself. Since God is greater than the capacity of the human mind, He always appears to be mysterious. The reality of God, even though it is faithfully grasped by notions that direct the mind toward God, does not offer it a lucid scientific clarity. It is better when the believer is given notions about faith that continue to be mysterious, but are true, than when clear and comprehensible notions are given that can be assimilated by the mind easily, but are false. Perseverance in faith always entails the acceptance of a certain obscurity of faith, locating its mystery in the life of the intellect, against which mental pride often rebels. This does not mean, however, that the mind is always so strongly blinded by faith that it is incapable of knowing anything about it and articulating it. Moreover, it does not mean that the mind in its natural functioning is wounded by faith.

The light of faith, as it persists in the soul, gives it a certain subjective seeing. This is not a simple vision of God, nor is it scientific knowledge. As a result of faith, a certain instinct of faith is born in the mind, which inclines toward adherence to that which truly is in accord with faith and is given for belief by the Church. It is only when one believes that one starts to understand certain things. A morally chaste person instinctively distinguishes chaste words and gestures from the unchaste, and so also a believing person, and in particular a person growing in faith, instinctively perceives whether a given claim is in accord with faith or not. This is a different type of discernment from that deriving from theological erudition, but it can give a strong light that will generate firm convictions, even when religious knowledge may be very poor. Sometimes an uneducated, but believing, individual hearing scholarly utterances about faith made on TV by an unbeliever will immediately sense an error, even though theological expertise that would allow for the precise location of the error or manipulation is lacking. Some people have a stronger instinct of faith than others. It depends on the temperament, but also upon the quality of prayer and openness toward the Holy Spirit.

Some people would like to reduce faith to a simple obedience understood as a subservience of the mind to imposed truth. They imagine that the merit of faith consists precisely in this subservience. This leads to the conclusion that God is not concerned about our thinking about the truthfulness of the assertions that are located in the mind and that He only wants our will, which is to be subdued and to accept blindly that what is taught in the Church. This was the accusation Calvin made against Catholics. The subject matter of faith is supposedly irrelevant, and so it may be ignored, so long as there is compliant subservience.

In such reasoning, the main emphasis is placed on the authority of the Church, which possesses the power to declare dogmas, and on the fact that they are binding, while the believer is expected to receive the faith formally without being bothered by it, without permitting that it will really influence thinking and life. What is then set aside is the fact that faith is the embracing of the human mind by God and the leading of it beyond its natural limit to the highest Truth. In reality, faith is the initiation of supernatural cognition that nourishes the soul, joining it to God, and so it orders thinking, including about matters that concern this world.

Faith is not an enemy of the mind, but an ally and a help leading to truths that are essential for the spiritual life. In faith there is some humility of the mind, but this humility, as it limits the mind's autonomous intellectual pride, is not a denial of the mind, which is still capable of raising questions and knowing truths both outside faith in the natural order and also within the mystery of faith. The limiting of the self-sufficiency of the mind by faith is not its mutilation. Reason, which is rational, is capable of knowing its limits and, precisely for this reason, can accept being drawn out to the deeper truth of faith. Because it is rational, it is not indifferent to whether the contents of faith that it is given to believe are true—exactly in accord with the deposit of faith that the Church has received—or whether they are false.

There are others who, reacting to the reduction of faith to obedience, place a major emphasis on the necessity of trust in faith, focusing more on this than on orthodox precision in the expressions of faith, which they deem to be unimportant. The precise articulation of dogmas by the Church is then treated not as a treasure, but as an unhappy necessity deriving probably from the current presence of heresies. There is a kernel of truth in this reaction, because faith, together with the other theological virtues, serves union with God. But this reaction has gone too far, leading to a sharp contradistinction between concepts and reality, between subjective experiences and dogmas, between that which is mystical and that which is formulated in a legal way, and between that which is attributed to life and that which belongs to institutions. In reality, faith needs a correct expression of its content, as the deposit of faith is handed down by the visible institutional Church through which the Holy Spirit is working. It is precisely this content that nourishes faith and defends it against deformation or its reduction to only an ephemeral, basically unessential emotion or premonition.

The dogmas of faith

The enunciations of faith that direct the adherence of the mind to God and that are transmitted through the Church are the articles of faith appearing in the creeds, also known as the dogmas of faith. In faith there are varying levels of clarity. Thus, some truths of faith are particularly difficult for the mind. For this reason, these truths have been collected in the symbols of faith, the creeds, and at length in the catechisms, so that the adherence of the intellect to the mysteries of faith will take place—but always motivated primarily by the authority of the disclosing God.

In the Creed the truth of faith is grasped through simple articles that cannot be reduced to one another. Each article of faith concerns a truth that in itself is not obvious and can be a certain obstacle for the mind. Nevertheless, the believer accepts it because it expresses the contents of faith that are transmitted by the Church.

Theology penetrates the contents of the articles of faith, trying to draw out their intelligibility, their internal meaning, and their consequences. It does not, however, prove the veracity of the articles of faith on the basis of some criteria that are extraneous to faith, which cannot be done, nor does it try to rework the articles so that they would fit human prejudices or expectations.

The biblical history of salvation covers many facts, and the evangelists' descriptions of the life of Jesus on earth contain many minute details. But the articles of faith grasp only that which is the most central, the essential content of truth, without denying the value of minor details, such as those concerning the miracles made by Jesus or His parables. This hierarchy among the truths of faith does not at all mean that some truths are less true than others. That would be a contradiction in terms. Each truth, if it is a truth, is as equally true as any other truth. The hierarchy of the truths of faith means only that some truths are more central for the faith than others. Faith in the Blessed Trinity is more fundamental than faith in the value of prayers for the dead, but this does not mean that praying for the deceased is pointless.

Historical studies demonstrate that there has been doctrinal development in the history of the Church. Some Catholics thought this to be unthinkable because they imagined that the deposit of faith had been transmitted in the same form from the very beginning. For centuries, it was held that the Apostles' Creed had been formulated by the apostles before they spread out in the world, and that each one of them remembered and transmitted one of the articles of this Creed. Today, it is known that the Apostles' Creed does not necessarily date back to apostolic times, but derives probably from the ancient baptismal liturgy of the Roman Church. As time progressed, additional creeds were formulated, and certain councils articulated the truths with greater precision. Since the Church has the deposit of faith from Christ that She passes on, why then is there a development in the transmitted contents of faith? Should not the deposit be unchanged in every respect?

Others are of the opinion that, since certainly there is a development of doctrine, we are bound only by the most recent ecclesial enunciations. Accordingly, they hope that, in time, even these will be replaced by something more facile. They ignore the earlier enunciations and think that it is possible to struggle in the Church, asking for a change of the troublesome doctrines. In the most important discourse of his pontificate, Benedict XVI reminded us that this is an erroneous approach. Vatican Council II must be read and interpreted in unison with the perennial teaching of the

Church and not treated as a revolutionary moment that changed the truths of faith.[30] It is true that there is doctrinal development in the history of the Church, but this does not entail a change of the deposit of faith, nor does it permit it. How then are we to interpret this development?

Just as the object of faith, that is the First Truth, is adapted somewhat to the capacity of the human mind so that it may adhere to the mystery of faith so, also, there is a certain adapting of the object of faith in the history of the Church. It is in this that doctrinal development is expressed. But is it then still the same object, since the adapting takes place within time, or does historical development permit diversity in the essentials? This question can also be drawn backward to the history of salvation. The gradual disclosure of the truth of faith by God dating back from the time of Abraham was a public, social fact that was conditioned historically. Did it, in the course of time, essentially change the contents of faith through which salvation takes place?

Undoubtedly there was a development of revelation before the coming of Christ. But in its *essence* everything was contained, even if implicitly, in the first revelation. Moses recognized in the burning bush that God exists and that He is concerned about us, and this is the most fundamental core of the salvific faith (Heb. 11:6). In the following centuries there was a gradual elucidation of the wealth contained in this divine providence, leading up to the Incarnation of the Son of God and the Redemption. Similarly, but not in the same way, after the reception of the fullness of revelation in Christ, we have witnessed a historical development in the penetration of the revealed truths. There is *no new revelation*, but the *expression*

[30] "Una giusta ermeneutica per leggere e recepire il Concilio come grande forza di rinnovamento della Chiesa," December 22, 2005, in *Insegnamenti di Benedetto XVI*, vol. 1 (Città del Vaticano, Libreria Editrice Vaticana, 2006), pp. 1018–1032.

of the faith is constantly deepened. The Church does this so as to distinguish the truth of faith from new heresies that appear, and also, as a result of meditating in faith, prayer, and reflection on the same mysteries of faith, in which the themes contained in them come to the fore.

Faith is infused in the soul by God, but the content of faith is transmitted by the Church. *Fides ex auditu* (see Rom. 10:17). Why does the Church intervene in the faith of individuals? We believe not *in view of* the Church, but *in view of* God, Who *makes use of* the Church to hand down the content of faith. This function of the Church is decisive, and it assures the exactitude of the subject matter offered to faith. During the era of the Church Fathers there was always an appeal to the "rule of faith," but this was understood not so much as a ruling for the faith of individuals imposed upon them by ecclesiastical authority, but as a rule that was the faith itself. This meant, above all, fidelity to the faith that was handed down by tradition, a fidelity that was binding also for Church authorities, bishops, and popes. The weight of tradition itself—that which has been passed on (1 Cor. 11:23), including the text of Holy Scriptures—is greater than the weight of the Church's Magisterium, which serves by explaining that tradition. It is therefore not surprising that over the centuries the declarations of the Church's Magisterium were scant. And when the Fathers spoke at the councils, they did not say, "We have decided that this will now be the belief," but rather, "Such is the faith of the Church that we confess." The new formulation was only a more precise articulation of that faith.

A dogmatic declaration is an articulation of the mysterious truth of faith that has been revealed by God and not by the Church. The Church's role is to focus the mind correctly toward God, our ultimate end and, thus, the plenitude of happiness. Dogmatic statements declare that a given truth belongs to the essence of faith, and so it nourishes thinking within faith and influences human life. Such a statement is infallibly declared by the appropriate authority of the teaching Church. But mystery within the truth of faith must not be forgotten. We cannot expect dogmatic truths to be convincing in themselves, nor that reason adheres to them with ease. In addition, we must not place too great an accent on the fact that a declaration is made by ecclesiastical authority. This attributes a juridical sense to the dogmas, suggesting that Church authorities are pressing down on the brakes of thinking. In fact, dogmatic declarations extend the mind further out, toward the life-giving mystery. They offer a deeper penetration of the revealed salvific truths.

Some people deem that if the Church has not spoken out on some issue, it is better not to think about it, because it is not known how things are. But once the Church has spoken, they claim that there is no point in thinking, because everything now is clear. The result is that it is better not to think at all! No, dogmatic statements are a gift given to the mind of the believer. Even though they are mysterious, they lead to the living God, Who cannot ever be understood completely, and so they illuminate the mind, forming the intellectual and moral life.

We can take as an example of this the two dogmatic statements of the Church about Mary: Her Immaculate Conception and Assumption. These two Marian dogmas, the first from 1854 and the second from 1950, were not announced in view of protecting the faith against some looming heresy. The awareness of their truth derived from the inner life of the Church, from the spirit of prayer and theological reflection undertaken within faith, in spite of the fact that biblical texts that speak of them directly cannot be shown. These two truths about the unique vocation of Mary—from the first instance of her existence to the end of her earthly life and her elevation, both body and soul, to Heaven—are an important point of reference for further theological reflection about the dignity of women. Mary did not become a goddess as a result of the Immaculate Conception. Her feminine humanity remained, as it had been in the initial divine project that preceded original sin. And her final elevation shows the end and purpose of that divine project. The declaration of these two dogmas, long before the appearance of contemporary feminism, can be seen to be providential because they offer a horizon for further thinking within faith on themes deriving from contemporary questions. A dogma is not therefore a brake imposed upon thinking. Rather, it is a course that leads that thinking toward the mystery that God disclosed for our salvation.

The deposit of faith that is preserved and transmitted in the Church is not a dead object that has been hidden somewhere in the cellar for many years. Rather, it nourishes the faith. That is why the rule, that is, the faith, is expressed also in the life, devotion, and experience of saints, and not only in precise theological formulas that appear later. One of the ways of expressing faith is the canonization of saints. We cannot, of course, say that the sanctity of a given saint was communicated in revelation. But the Church knows from revelation what sanctity is, and so She recognizes it infallibly among her members, and points to it. Thus, the teaching that is given with the canonization of saints focuses faith toward the life-giving mystery.

Right from the beginning, the Church has been nourished by the Eucharist. Only at a later stage were the Gospels written, and centuries later came dogmatic declarations about the Eucharist that used the newly coined term "transubstantiation." But transubstantiation was always taking place, right from the Last Supper, whenever the Eucharist was celebrated in the Church. The deposit of faith does not, therefore, grow over the centuries because the Church does not receive some new and continuous revelation. The Church articulates the already given truths of faith, but with greater precision—and yet they always are, and remain, mysterious. The dogma of transubstantiation protects faith in the reality of the Eucharist, but it does not make it comprehensible according to our natural thinking.

It happens sometimes that some truths of faith seem to be forgotten. Then they are excavated from the treasures or the memory of the Church. When practical pastoral teaching was too concentrated on moral obligation and natural human effort, St. Thérèse of Lisieux pointed to the way of trustful love of the loving Father, and St. Faustina Kowalska spoke about mercy as the greatest divine attribute. This brought about a correction. These two saints did not reveal new truths of faith, but rather they brought out truths that already were part of the deposit of faith, even though they had been forgotten or shelved. Private revelations, therefore, are not in the indicative but in the imperative tense. They bring out truths that already exist in the treasures of the Church that merit attention. Similarly, doctrinal declarations of the Church express with greater precision the salvific truths that are part of the deposit of faith when the situation needs this.

In the formulation of doctrinal declarations, the Church strives for an enunciation of the salvific truth that will separate it from erroneous notions that are present in society and that sometimes are very fashionable and politically correct. It is not surprising, therefore, that holding on to the truth has often generated resistance. But the Church is not bothered by this because the Church knows that She is a sign that is rejected (see Luke 2:34).

This effort of the Catholic Church differs essentially from what for centuries the Church of England has tried to work out. There, in moments of conflict, most often what was sought were more general expressions, that in principle had to be so vague that all could interpret them in their own way, finding in them what was pleasing to them. In place of a pope who transmits the deposit of faith, the Anglican Church has the office of a primate, whose main task consists in negotiating between contrary currents and working out basically meaningless compromises. Within the Anglican Communion, widely differing dogmatic and moral positions coexist. They are joined together on the basis of the famous English spirit of compromise. Elegantly formulated statements that are unclear from the start may momentarily gather together differing social groups within one community. This has a political meaning, but it does not lead to a deepening and awakening of faith, but only to its gradual decline because this reduces religiosity to banality and generates moral relativism. The Church of England, which has an established political and legal position, is united not by a confessed doctrinal and moral truth, but by the need of the British Crown. For centuries it gave religious legitimacy and a certain Christian dignity to the legal and civil order of the state and the British Empire. But to the extent that British society is becoming irreligious and multicultural, affirming motley ideologies that are very distant from Christianity, the British state and the states of the former colonies are expecting from Anglicanism increasingly less support. That is why diametrically contradictory dogmatic and moral positions are exploding that community from within.

Catholicism does not permit declarations of the truths of faith to be imprecise from the start. Dogmas articulated by the Church have to express authentically the same faith that the Church has received, distinguishing it from falsehood, because this faith is leading the Church toward eternity. Forced by nascent errors, the Church at times arrived at a grasping of the truth in its greater plenitude and drew essential conclusions from this truth that earlier had not been noticed. In this effort the Church has had recourse to human concepts deriving from the current culture or philosophical trends. Sometimes the declarations of the faith were made in response to some very concrete difficulty that had appeared in a given moment, and so they employed the terminology and the knowledge of the times. These doctrinal declarations were located within some scientific presuppositions, exegetical interpretations, or views of history, all of which do not belong to the rule of faith. The final declaration of faith is based not on them but on the assistance of the Holy Spirit. It is not, therefore, surprising that the interpretation of doctrinal statements from distant centuries requires some finesse and the ability to identify that which is historically conditioned and, accordingly, does not belong to the deposit of faith.

The declaration of dogmas that grasp the truth of faith is a sign not of the Church's narrow-mindedness but of her pastoral concern. It is a confirmation of the truth so that the minds of the faithful adhere to the mystery of faith. It was never a case of announcing new truths, but only their renewed expression. And so always there was some progress in this. Sometimes, during theological disputes, the Church refrained from taking a position because it was noted that the issue had not matured sufficiently to warrant a declaration. It was deemed better to wait until the matter had been prayed about and studied in depth. The Church has time, and so this waiting sometimes lasts for centuries. Moreover, the way of declaring truths of faith is subject to change. The Second Vatican Council moved away from making short statements and anathemas that excluded erroneous thinking, even though this procedure was used by earlier councils. A more descriptive, positive, lengthy exposition, sensitive toward contemporary resistances in an attempt to unknot miscomprehensions concerning the faith, was projected to accompany today's faithful more effectively. Such an approach has pastoral value, but it also is subject to misunderstanding. On this occasion, the Church has said that truth itself, expressed in faith and charity, will draw people more than a cold and sharp distinction between falsehood and truth.

Pondering the mysteries of faith

It is important that faith be correct. The Church ensures this by handing down the content of faith that had been received and conserved through tradition. When this content is studied, in order to penetrate its meaning and to search for internal connections and reasons, not only is it received as true, but also one *understands* what one believes. This is always an enrichment of faith. Faith may exist without such an intellectual cognitive effort, but then "the head is empty,"[31] and so, as a result, faith has little influence on thinking, deciding, or the wider culture. The studied contents of faith should not, however, be treated as a closed conceptual system that can be easily received by the mind, which then embarks upon unrestricted mental adventures, similar to logical deductions or mathematical operations. The content of faith cannot be locked in logical premises from which all conclusions could be exhaustively drawn out by way of syllogisms. However, this does not mean that one cannot reflect upon the contents of faith in a logical way. Faith always accepts that which is not evident because it leads toward the mystery, and the subject matter of a mystery cannot be exhausted completely.

By focusing the mind on both dogmatic and moral truths deduced from revelation, faith leads one closer to the living Person of Jesus Christ, the incarnate eternal Word of the Father. A living person who is also a divine Person is a reality more profound than any knowledge, even the most advanced and precise scientific knowledge. That is why, referring to the Fourth Lateran Council and to St. Thomas Aquinas, the *Catechism of the Catholic Church* reminds us:

> Likewise, we must recall that "between Creator and creature no similitude can be expressed without implying an even

[31] St. Thomas Aquinas, *Quodlibet* IV, q. 9, art. 3.

> greater dissimilitude"; and that "concerning God, we cannot grasp what He is, but only what He is not, and how other beings stand in relation to Him." (43)

The human mind, even within faith, has to be accustomed to the fact that it is limited and incapable of understanding everything exhaustively when it reaches out toward God. When the mind adheres to God through faith, it receives the living mystery of God, Who encompasses us with His love and Who, in His eternal project, has planned the divine filiation for us in His Son. St. Paul was very much aware of this when it dawned upon him that he had "been entrusted with this special grace, not only of proclaiming to the pagans the infinite treasure of Christ, but also of explaining how the mystery is to be dispensed. Through all the ages, this has been kept hidden in God, the Creator of everything" (Eph. 3:8–9).

The humble reception of the divine mystery through faith elicits openness to the paternity of God and to the filiation given by Him. It is possible to grow in a childlike relationship with God, when one allows oneself to be led by the Holy Spirit and so to live according to the inner life of God (Rom. 8:14). When, however, the individual is locked in rational thinking that becomes more important than faith, there is a focus on self, and this generates an inclination to impose one's own ideas upon God. This destroys openness to divine paternity, to filiation, and to being led by the Holy Spirit.

The content of faith known from revelation and transmitted by the Church will always be mysterious. It is to be received as such, and yet it may still play a leading role in the life of the mind. It is precisely in receiving it that one is rooted, united to God, thanks to which one is not "tossed one way and another and carried along by every wind of doctrine, at the mercy of all the tricks men play and their cleverness in practicing deceit" (Eph. 4:14). That is why

St. Paul wrote that by "kneeling before the Father" and, even more so, by bending his mind to the received mystery, in this act of faith he united in prayer with God, pleading that He would "give you the power through His Spirit for your hidden self to grow strong." His hope encompassed the entire intellectual and spiritual life of those who would read his letters. "Christ may live in your hearts through faith, and then, planted in love and built on love, you will with all the saints have strength to grasp the breadth and the length, the height and the depth; until, knowing the love of Christ, which is beyond all knowledge, you are filled with the utter fullness of God" (Eph. 3:14–19). He wanted the received mystery of the risen Lord, the Son, and Word of God—that is, the mystery of the divine project—to seize the minds of believers, granting breadth to their horizons, an extensive view full of perseverant hope, one that is from the height of Christ's Cross and has depth resulting from openness to the assisting power of the Holy Spirit.

St. John of the Cross referred to this deeper and deeper penetration of Christ and the truth about Him when he compared Him to "an abundant mine with many recesses of treasures, so that however deep individuals may go they will never reach the end or bottom."[32] We can modernize this image by comparing this pondering to the unpacking of a computer program. We normally use only a small percentage of a program that is already installed in our computer. When we have to do something new, we discover that our computer program allows for a new operation, and then there is a moment of joy. Similarly, as we probe the truths of faith that are important for our lives, we discover their richness. We have faith from Baptism, and the Church directs it, but when we discover further dimensions of the unimaginable depth that is Christ, there is always a moment of joy. Thinking within faith

[32] *Spiritual Canticle*, stanza 37, 4, in *Collected Works*, pp. 615–616.

discloses new dimensions of the divine mystery, but it never ceases to be a mystery.

We can compare the attitude of the Church toward the truths of faith to that of Mary, about whom the Gospel says that she "treasured all these things and pondered them in her heart" (Luke 2:19, also 1:29; 2:51). This reflective pondering entails something more than intellectual cognition, the working through a logical deduction, or the inventing of something new. The Church has received in faith the binding deposit that opens us up toward the mystery. She treasures it with love, and, when there is a need, She draws out of it hitherto unnoticed riches. Importantly, She always remembers that it is not a mere satisfaction of intellectual cognitive curiosity, but an encounter with the living God, provoking an effusion of His grace that happens whenever faith formed by charity is directed toward Him.

This Marian pondering going on in the Church over the ages contains within itself the seed of doctrinal development, because through it, as the years and centuries pass, the treasures contained in the mystery of faith are unearthed. Blessed John Henry Newman described this in a conference given at the University in Oxford:

> Thus St. Mary is our pattern of faith, both in the reception and in the study of Divine Truth. She does not think it enough to accept it, she dwells upon it; not enough to possess, she uses it; not enough to assent, she develops it; not enough to submit the Reason, she reasons upon it; not indeed reasoning first, and believing afterwards, with Zacharias, yet first believing without reasoning, next from love and reverence, reasoning after believing. And thus she symbolizes to us, not only the faith of the unlearned, but of the doctors of the Church also, who have to investigate, and weigh, and define, as well as to profess the Gospel; to draw

the line between truth and heresy; to anticipate or remedy the various aberrations of wrong reason; to combat pride and recklessness with their own arms; and thus to triumph over the sophist and the innovator.[33]

[33] *Sermon* XV, 3, in *Fifteen Sermons Preached before the University of Oxford* (Notre Dame, IN: University of Notre Dame Press, 1997), pp. 313–314.

4

Reason and Faith — Unmixed

Chalcedon

The Council of Chalcedon in 451 clarified that as we confess our faith in Jesus Christ, we must acknowledge His two natures, human and divine, "without confusion or change, without division or separation."[34] Both divinity and humanity are in Jesus complete, unmutilated, with no separating schizophrenia that would suggest that Jesus was at times a man and at others God. There is no dilution of Jesus' humanity within His divinity or of His divinity within His humanity. The true divinity of the Son of God has been disclosed and is available to us in the full, true, glorified humanity of Jesus. In the Church, it is such a Jesus who is simultaneously God and man that we confess.

The conciliar emphasis of the fact that the two natures in Jesus are unmixed (*asynkhytos*) and inseparable may be applied also to the mind of the believer. Within the believer there has to be a place both for reason and for faith, and they are not to be confused;

[34] *The Christian Faith in the Doctrinal Documents of the Catholic Church*, ed. J. Neuner and J. Dupuis (New York: Alba House, 2001), no. 615.

if such confusion were to occur, it would not be known whether the mind hosted faith or knowledge.[35] Furthermore, reason and faith are not to be kept too apart, as this would imply that these two orders of cognition function in total conflict with one another, or in an absolutely parallel and mutually indifferent fashion. This would point to a kind of schizophrenia. Both reason and faith have their own dignity, each within its order, and they need to respect one another. Since faith is not based on rational arguments but on the authority of the self-revealing God, Who does not lie, this means that confessing the faith, growing in it, deepening the encounter with God, and becoming increasingly susceptible to the workings of grace, through faith, require that the reason of the believer cedes the prime place to faith.

By no means is this obvious for the rational faculty, because reason readily stops short at the level of its own, autonomous and proud self-sufficiency. Reason then succumbs to the temptation of arranging some simple compromise with faith. This may happen when faith is respectfully declared but, in fact, is treated as an irrelevant external veneer that has no real bearing on thinking and practical morality. In this way, faith is expelled from the intellectual life and transferred to the sphere of fleeting emotions, feelings, and sentiments, while skepticism is maintained in the sphere of reason, leading to a purely circumstantial approach to life's decisions. It also may happen that faith is intermingled with reason to such an extent that it ceases to be itself, that it no longer entails openness to the divine mystery and becomes some form of knowledge, subordinated to its criteria. And, finally, it may turn out that there is such a sharp parting of reason and faith that the reason functions completely independently, treating faith as

[35] M.-J. Le Guillou, *Le mystère du Père: Foi des apôtres, Gnoses actuelles* (Paris: Fayard, 1972).

irrelevant, and absolutely rejecting the notion that there may also be a place for faith within it and that thinking within faith is justified. This then results in ceding primacy to the sciences, including philosophy, and the rejection of theology or, even worse, the disdainful treatment of theology as some fake, untrue reflection that is beneath the dignity of reason.

The individuation of these multiple protests of reason against faith is important, because their naming allows for the liberation of the mind from unconscious resistances against faith that prevent it from permeating deeply one's psyche and life. Faith and reason have to work out their mutual relationship, but this has to be done in a Chalcedonian way. Reason and faith are not to be mutilated, nor are they to be radically separated, because this results in the marginalization of faith and theology, leading to the rejection of thinking within faith, or to their intermingling in such a way that faith is subordinated to reason. It is essential that faith be always based on God alone, and not on human arguments. It is only then that the primacy of the encounter with the living God and openness to His grace are maintained. It is better to become aware of the primacy of faith and of the consequences flowing from this, even though the confession of faith requires the humility of reason, than simply to *pretend* that faith is most important while its role in the psyche and spiritual life is deformed or marginalized.

Unfortunately, both ancient and contemporary Gnostics easily blend the discourses of faith and reason. They freely switch between philosophy and theology, treating them as basically identical. Always, whenever there is such intermingling, faith is distorted. Gnosticism is an attempt to transform faith so that it becomes knowledge. It subjects the revealed truths of faith to external interpretations, assessing them in the light of assumptions that are beyond the mystery of faith. When one tries to pick and choose amongst the truths of faith and to justify or to single out only those fragments of the divine mystery that are deemed worthy of accepting—and when this is done through reference to criteria derived from this world—the mystery of faith is subordinated to purely human standards and ideas. This happens, irrespective of whether the criteria are furnished by philosophy, linguistics, archaeology, history, comparative studies of religions, astronomy, psychology and political sciences, ideologies that are treated as unshakable, politically correct social programs, or even personal projects and subjective convictions about pastoral relevancy. If these turn out to be decisive, then faith is cut short. When we conclude that the truths of faith ultimately are nothing different from what is asserted by these sciences based on their cognitive methodologies, or that the challenges deriving from faith are identical to some political ideologies and precisely and only for this reason are they accepted, then such a simple concordism of faith with knowledge or human projects destroys faith.

Attempts to rework faith so as to make it credible and relevant according to the world's standards, which then become its ultimate justification, lead directly to a distortion of faith. Faith is then revised and conformed to human measures and ideals. In such a chaotic entanglement of knowledge and faith, faith becomes confused and does not know what it believes in view of God, what it knows on the basis of natural science, what it accepts because it is fashionable, and what it only suspects in a human way. In the Gnostic approach the mind no longer confesses the received truth and does not grow within it. It only enjoys its own knowledge, and the more complex it is, the more the mind is proud of its unique, purely rational cognition and supposedly scientific *Weltanschauung*, or worldview.

This basic presupposition excludes initiation into the living mystery of God. The mind remains closed within some kind of reductionism and is unable to reach out to the fullness of truth generously disclosed in the Word of God. At most, some fragment of it is accepted, and only the one that is found pleasing. There is a picking and choosing within truth like that of a shopper in a supermarket, who takes some goods and leaves others. The revealed truths are viewed at most as one more argument that may or may not be taken into consideration. The true believer recognizes that an essential shift has taken place and that in such a supposedly religious discourse that has, in fact, been subordinated to human criteria, the true light of God has been extinguished.

In reality, in the life of faith, the revealed truths are not filtered through the sieve of scientific, ideological, or personal criteria, but instead, the exact opposite happens. In a living faith, one's own life is assessed by the supreme criterion that is the revealed truth, given to us in its fullness in the Paschal Mystery of Jesus Christ. We believe God, because God has spoken and has allowed us to enter into a relationship with Him—on His conditions, not ours. The self-disclosing God is the basic object of faith and, at the same time, its fundamental and unique motive. When we believe God *in view of God* we allow Him, and so also the entire revealed truth, to permeate our mind, our intellectual life, our culture, our decision-making, our morals, and our affectivity.

Accepting as the ultimate principle of thinking the unmutilated, uninvented, untampered Paschal Mystery of Jesus Christ—that is, His redemptive Passion, death, and Resurrection, granting the grace of Holy Spirit—for the sole reason that it is the uninvited entry of God into our lives, may seem to be supremely odd. But it is with precisely such a key that we need to think and to act in faith. This is the ultimate hermeneutic principle that Jesus gave to us, calling all those who do not follow it foolish (Luke 24:25). The two disciples on the way to Emmaus honestly expressed their human hopes, imaginings, and political ideas concerning the Messiah, and since it was these that were decisive for them, after the Crucifixion they were completely downcast. Jesus explained to them that both the Scriptures and their own projects have to be read in the light of that unique key that is the eternal project of the heavenly Father, which was made manifest in the Paschal Mystery. "Was it not ordained that the Christ should suffer and so enter into His glory?" (Luke 24:26). The human mind is to be always open toward the divine mystery that was disclosed in the redemptive work of Jesus, even though that mystery cannot be fully understood and exhaustively known.

It is worth noting that St. Paul also used the word "foolish" when he criticized the Galatians, or rather the missionaries who followed him to Galatia and deformed the purity of the faith. They had insisted that the new converts from paganism were to function according to the instructive rules of the Jewish tradition and external Law, and not on the basis of faith centered on Christ. "Are you people in Galatia mad?" (Gal. 3:1).

St. Paul clearly distinguished between human traditions, ideas, and achievements—among which are located the Jewish tradition and Greek philosophy, the natural value of which he never denied—and the divine faith that opens us to grace. He had no doubt that ultimately we are to follow faith and not autonomous and proud reason and its ideas. He insisted therefore: "In my speeches and the sermons I gave, there were none of the arguments that belong to philosophy; only a demonstration of the power of the Spirit. And I did this so that your faith should not depend on human philosophy but on the power of God" (1 Cor. 2:4–5).

In his concern, the apostle wrote "to stir your minds, so that your understanding may come to full development, until you really know God's secret" (Col. 2:2). He therefore warned: "Make sure that no one traps you and deprives you of your freedom, by some secondhand, empty, rational philosophy based on the principles of this world instead of Christ" (Col. 2:8). St. Paul not only insisted that the faithful were to avoid Sophist intellectual aberrations. He also cautioned them against even good philosophy, such as the Greeks', which rightly strives to arrive at the truth known rationally, when it becomes the unique and final criterion of thinking and life, thereby extinguishing faith.[36]

One of the Cappadocian Fathers, St. Gregory of Nazianzus, expressed himself in a similar way. He demonstrated that when faith is recognized as being fundamental, it does not impede the reason, but, in fact, develops it. But the primacy of faith needs to be maintained:

> For when we leave off believing, and protect ourselves by mere strength of argument, and destroy the claim which the Spirit has upon our faith by questionings, and then our argument is not strong enough for the importance of the subject (and this must necessarily be the case, since it is put in motion by an organ of so little power as is our mind), what is the result? The weakness of the argument appears to belong to the mystery, and thus elegance of language makes void the Cross, as Paul also thought [1 Cor. 1:17]. For faith is that which completes our argument.[37]

[36] This is how St. Thomas Aquinas understood these words of St. Paul. Being both an outstanding philosopher and a theologian, Aquinas knew how to distinguish clearly between the order of nature and grace, and so between philosophical cognition and the thinking in faith that is appropriate for the sacred teaching of theology. I wrote about this in my book *Rachunek sumienia teologii moralnej* (The examination of conscience of moral theology), (Kraków: Wydawnictwo M, 2004), pp. 169–178.

[37] *Oration* 29, 21 in *Nicene and Post-Nicene Fathers*, Second Series, vol. 7, trans. Charles Gordon Browne and James Edward Swallow, ed. Philip Schaff and Henry Wace (Buffalo, NY: Christian Literature, 1894), revised and edited for New Advent by Kevin Knight, http://www.newadvent.org/fathers/310229.htm.

When the primacy of faith is recognized by reason, the mind is not wounded; whereas reason wounds faith whenever it attributes primacy to itself. Faith sharpens perception, leading reason to the truth. It also grants certitude that has its origin in the Cross of Christ. Furthermore, the exercise of faith habituates in the employment of grace gushing from the Cross into the moral life, and so it does not empty grace of its power by ignoring it or expelling it from the psyche, as happens whenever the reason thinks that it is self-sufficient—that it does not need grace and therefore despises it. Faith is not based on human argumentation but on God Himself. It does, of course, happen that the motives of faith intermingle, and sometimes lower reasons seem to be decisive for faith. For many people, parental authority, the heritage of one's culture, apologetic arguments, or hearing about naturally inexplicable miracles are such motives. These may *seem* to be decisive, but as faith is deepened, the adherence to God—Himself, the First Truth, in view of Himself, made possible due to grace—starts to outweigh them with absolute force. And we need to persist in this adherence to God in view of Him.

The belief of the Samaritans from Sychar mentioned in the Gospel was an occasion for the following comment of Aquinas:

> Now faith is right when it obeys the truth not for some alien reason, but for the truth itself; and as to this he [the evangelist] says that *they said to the woman, now we believe*, the truth, *not just because of your story*, but because of the truth itself. Three things lead us to believe in Christ. First of all, natural reason ... second, the testimony of the law and the prophets ... third, the preaching of the apostles and others.... Yet when a person, having been thus instructed, believes, he can then say that it is not for any of these reasons that he believes: i.e., neither on account of natural reason, nor the

> testimony of the law, nor the preaching of others, but solely on account of the truth itself.[38]

It is God Who grants the grace of faith and causes the reason to adhere to the mystery revealed by Him. Faith may also be prompted by human arguments. What is decisive, however, is the reception of the grace of faith and persistence in it in view of God—on the basis of the received divine light, even if initially that faith appears to be pale and fragile. It is true that the content of faith is transmitted by the Church, but this does not change the fact that faith adheres to the living, that is, mysterious and revealed, God, in view of Himself, and not because of the authority of the Church or of the witness of even the most pleasing preacher.

The explanation offered by the sixteenth-century Jesuit theologian Luis Molina, who claimed that natural faith is essentially indistinct from supernatural faith given by grace, is erroneous. He held that although the object of faith is God, its motive is always natural, not supernatural. According to him, grace only facilitates *the execution of acts of faith*, just as oil eases the functioning of a machine. In essence, he claimed that faith is just a simple epistemological fact—the reception of that which does not immediately appear as evident—and that this is done for purely natural reasons. Either the grounds for faith have been explained in a process of natural reasoning that has ultimately been recognized as convincing, or simply one holds that belief is in some way necessary.[39] This explanation undercuts the supernatural character of faith. Faith is a divine gift that enables the encounter of human nature with the

[38] *Super Evangelium S. Ioannis lectura*, c. 4, l. 2 (662), in *Commentary on the Gospel of John, Chapters 1–8*, trans. Fabian R. Larcher (Lander, WY: Aquinas Institute for the Study of Sacred Doctrine, 2013), p. 247.

[39] Dulles, *The Assurance of Things Hoped For*, pp. 55, 226.

living supernatural God and opens to His grace, but in Molina's view, even though faith is directed toward God, it is reduced to the level of a natural mental process in which that which is not supported by empirical or logical proofs is accepted as true. This is the same as treating as true the supposition that there are no nails in a bar of chocolate and so it may be bitten without any preceding scientific investigation.

Such a naturalistic interpretation of the functioning and motive of faith—perhaps spawned by the Renaissance fascination with nature, natural religiosity, and philosophy—had to lead to treating faith not as a mystical moment that ignites the movement of divine grace within the soul, but as a moment of natural trust based on human arguments or moral obligation. This view of faith generates, of course, understandable resistances. If what is perceived in faith is only a transfer from the hearing of arguments to trustful belief, undertaken because supposedly logic demands it or because it is somehow obligatory—meaning that the move is produced by natural forced effort—then obviously further questions are raised. Why, if reason is more important, do we *have* to believe when faith tells us what in itself is not obvious? In this interpretation of faith there is no place for the encounter with the living God on the basis of His gift, in view of Himself and His promises. Thus, openness to grace vanishes. What only remains is the sad necessity of putting a brake on the natural *eros* of the reason by faith.

Once again, it may be noticed that the exaggerated elevation of the reason by the philosophy of the Enlightenment, tied with the reduction of faith to the level of a meaningless superstition, was in fact the result of the limitations of earlier, Baroque-period theology. This theological current insufficiently brought out the interpersonal union of man with God and excessively stressed moral obligation, but with no initiation into the spiritual life. Moral teaching that was void of mysticism and the encounter with the living God, and a faith that ignored grace and was based on supposedly natural reasons, finally generated the rebellion of the Enlightenment.

This explanation of faith that slipped from the supernatural level—igniting the movement of grace in the soul—to the level of a purely natural epistemological fact located somewhere in between an opinion, a judgment, a supposition, a conclusion, and an assertion made on the basis of a moral obligation, was tied with another shift in theological thought: The place in the eternal divine plan of attributing a *filial status* to humans was also moved.

In His mission and Paschal Mystery, Jesus disclosed the original divine intent, the *Logos*, for us. From the very beginning God had planned that we would become children of the heavenly Father through our Brother Jesus Christ. This divine project precedes the creation of the cosmos and our coming into existence. It also precedes sin, both that of Adam and our own. St. Paul stated clearly that "before the world was made, [God] chose us . . . to live through love in His presence, determining that we should become His adopted sons, through Jesus Christ" (Eph. 1:4–5).

To be a child of God means to live according to the inner life of God Himself. This becomes possible, because "everyone moved by the Spirit of God is a son of God" (Rom. 8:14). Furthermore, it entails the liberation from a fearful feeling of unworthiness, because as adopted children we can relate to God in an intimate and familial way, crying out, "*Abba*, Father!" (Rom. 8:15). When Jesus wanted to bring home the perspective of our living according to the same Spirit who animates the relationships between the divine Persons, He made the following comparison: "I know my own [sheep] and my own know me, just as the Father knows me and I know the Father" (John 10:14–15). It follows that such an intimate relationship as exists between the Father and the Son is planned also for us as we relate with Jesus. This is to happen not only in a distant eternity, as a reward for our good behavior, but also here on earth as we live by faith and charity. This bond has been planned for us by God since before the creation of the world. St. Peter taught us that we do not have to be paralyzed by this perspective and think that sin has excluded us from it, because "the ransom that was paid to free you ... was ... in the precious blood of a Lamb without spot or stain, namely Christ; who, though known since before the world was made, has been revealed only in our time" (1 Pet. 1:18–20).

Unfortunately, a current of thought appeared in Catholic theology that transferred the original divine project of our filiation in Christ to a time *after* creation and *after* sin, presenting it as a divine response to the Fall of man.[40] This led to the treatment of creation, as well as the cosmos and its nature, as a self-standing reality, a "pure nature" that can be studied by an autonomous reason, completely free from the influence of faith. In the meantime, the perspective of the mystical encounter with God was referred to a distant eschatology or to an extraordinary sphere that does not touch the ordinary man.

In such a perspective, *divine creative omnipotence* overshadows *divine paternity*. The cosmos came to be understood as a self-explanatory fact or as a result of impersonal divine potency, and not

[40] We find a suggestion of such a shift already in St. Augustine. See St. Augustine, *The Lord's Sermon on the Mount* I, 23, trans. J. J. Jepson, Ancient Christian Writers, vol. 5 (New York: Newman Press, 1948), p. 89: "We, therefore, become sons of God by a spiritual rebirth and are adopted into the kingdom of God not as though we were strangers, but as made and created by Him. Thus there is the one kindness, His having created us by His almighty power when before we were nothing; and the other, whereby He adopted us that as sons we might enjoy with Him eternal life to the measure of our participation." Hence He did not say: "Do these things because you are children"; but: "Do these things in order that you may be children." But in reality the divine project of our filiation precedes creation.

as a gift of the heavenly Father. Thus nature, including human nature, was viewed as being free and divorced from grace. Grace was understood to be an extraordinary, optional, and unnecessary gift. This, among other things, led to the study of morality uniquely on the basis of philosophical reflection, with reference to the natural law, but unmoored from grace, from spirituality, from openness to the paternal love of God.

The paternity of God may be recognized in faith within the Paschal Mystery of Jesus. If the love of the Father, expressed through the gift of self of His Son, who had been sent, is not perceived, then what is noticed in the death of Jesus is only the fact that He was condemned and executed. This leads to concentration on one's own ideas and hopes, which ends in discouragement, as it did for the disciples on the way to Emmaus. The attribution of primacy to personal ideas, and so the placing of individual reason above the pilgrimage of faith, ends in the imposition upon reality of one's own ideological or scientific projects. As a result, one falls out of a filial relationship with God. The encounter with the living God, Who disclosed to us His paternal personal countenance in Christ, "the image of the unseen God" (Col. 1:15), becomes impossible when purely human thinking reigns in the mind, rather than the *Logos*, the Word that became flesh. When our own ideals turn out to be more important than the divine Word received in faith, they become the ultimate criterion of thinking, and they witness not to Christ, but to self. And in thinking about morality, what then is in the center is not the force of Christ's grace enabling the living out of the demands of divine charity, but only an attempt to adapt the Christian moral perspective to the limited capacities of a weak and wounded human nature.

As the Chalcedonian principle is applied to our thinking, we must ensure that the divine mystery—received in faith for the sole motive of the self-revealing God—has a central place in the mind and that it influences practical life. This mystery of faith is distinct and it has to remain such, unmixed with the conclusions of a purely naturally functioning mind. This does not mean, however, that the natural mind is to disappear.

Faith does not destroy reason

Faith does not destroy reason because even within faith itself, there is room for thinking. The act of faith is defined as *thinking with assent,* which means that in a mature faith, formed by charity, this thinking is a well-disposed and grateful pondering. By nature the human intellect is intent to know, and when it knows something, it wants to know it better, in depth and precision. This happens also within faith.

Faith is the descent of God toward man. This is the most important and basic fact about faith. In it, as in the other theological virtues of hope and charity, the human faculties are mastered by God. God as First Truth becomes accessible to the human mind through the gift of faith, which adapts the mind so that it may receive the First Truth. Similarly, hope is the divine focusing of the will toward the mystery that is unfolding in life, and through which God is leading the person. Charity is the supernatural adapting of the will, so that the individual may befriend God and then transfer that friendly relationship with Him onto others, who are also friends of God.

God's overpowering of the human faculties does not entail the denial of these faculties. If God were to switch off the natural capacities of reason and the authenticity of the working of the will, faith would then be reduced to fideism—a thoughtless, unfree assent to the revealed truth. This would then allow for contradictions. The attitude that claims: "I believe, because it is absurd" is wrong. Faith does not deny the possibility of thinking and of a real cognition of truth both beyond faith and within it. It only nudges the thinking further, toward the received truth. This takes place under the influence of the will, which assents to this extended thinking and even urges it on. Is this intervention of the will in the functioning of the mind justified?

In faith there is a paradox. The adherence to the revealed truth by faith comes about only because it is willed. The will itself does not move toward the truth but, rather, to the good. But in faith, the voice of the witness, God, urges the will from within by grace, and then the will recognizes the supreme Good in the First Truth. Accordingly, the will prompts the intellect to receive the truth of faith. What is central in faith is that the will, which is inclined toward the good, experiences a spontaneous movement toward God, the supreme Good. We can even advance the thesis that the internal aspiration of the will inclines the intellect to search for traces of such a revelation that would offer redemption from evil and allow one to strive for the good.[41] This is not a purely subjective derailment of cognition by a stubborn exercise of the will; rather, it is the keen yearning of the will for that supreme good that the will naturally desires with the added note that in faith this desire of the will is strengthened from within by grace. The will therefore does not appear in faith as a force that distrusts the intellect and imposes a brake upon it, but rather the exact opposite: The will urges the intellect to go forward courageously, without searching for excuses that would validate its withdrawal from faith. It invites the intellect to reach out toward the supreme Truth that is located beyond the natural cognitive capacities of the intellect. In faith, God is the *object* of faith as the First Truth. At the same time, He is also its *motive*, as the supreme Good. That

[41] Dulles, *The Assurance of Things Hoped For*, p. 212.

Good draws the will, which then awakens the intellect, so that it will accept the Truth.

This means that faith is not located uniquely in the cognitive order. It encompasses the entire person, involving also the will, which shows the intellect that it is good for it to adhere to God. In faith, therefore, there is some openness toward the eschatological perspective, to which the will is inclined as it desires the supreme Good and extends beyond the limits of this world. Thus, in faith there is a certain affective, very humane moment. The act of belief is too personal an issue to come about uniquely on the basis of purely logical rational arguments. In credence there is the free acceptance of that which has been proposed by a witness that is trusted. This corresponds to the normal human experience of trusting people. But in supernatural faith, that witness is God Himself, whom we trust and in whom we recognize the supreme Good. Other witnesses, like the evangelical Samaritan woman, are secondary in faith. They lead toward belief in the basic Witness, who has spoken in revelation and who touches us personally.

Faith grants certitude based on this initial credence, but it leaves a certain hunger, because the intellect that desires to know continues to think, and it wants to know more and with greater certitude. Thus, in faith there is still a place for searching, for asking questions, for engaging in an internal mental discourse. The reason sometimes experiences some discomfort in this seeking, because it is aware that engagement in faith requires a certain dose of courage. Meanwhile faith is dark, and the reason would prefer light, making everything clear. The obscurity of faith, however, is normal, because faith is an encounter with the mystery. God hides in a mystery so that we would know Him in faith, and not through proud knowledge, because only where there is faith may love be born. Where there is only clear knowledge, without trust, love cannot be born. That is why faith, including that of the great mystics, is always dark. To love God, we have to receive Him in faith, for no other reason apart from Himself. And if within faith, other motives have become dominant, over time they will have to be purified, so that faith increasingly will be based on God alone and nourished only by Him.

The psychological process of the act of faith in which the intellect and the will are engaged, urged from within by grace, does not in any way undercut the natural capacities of the mind. The normal functioning of reason within philosophy and the other sciences is still fully justified—even though it does not lead to salvation. A believing individual may be an expert in some field and his faith will not be an obstacle in his scientific research. Conflicts with faith are born only when science goes beyond its limits, when it starts to speak out on themes that are not in its field of competence and when in an ideological manner it proposes some substitute form of salvation. Reason is not deposed by faith. But if it attributes primacy—that is, the capacity to give ultimate answers about salvation—to itself, and if it considers itself entitled to speak about the living God on the basis of its own arguments and reasons, then faith requires that it be dethroned. When reason knows its place, its natural capacities are respected by faith and even enhanced. What's more, faith that is open to the revealed truth impels reason so that using its own methods it will strive for the fullness of truth. In the encyclical *Fides et ratio*, in which St. John Paul II viewed reason engaged in philosophy from the perspective of faith (Is not this the only way in which a pope speaks out?), he courageously wrote:

> In the light of faith which finds in Jesus Christ this ultimate meaning [of life], I cannot but encourage philosophers … to trust in the power of human reason and not to set themselves goals that are too modest in their philosophizing.…

> This is the path to follow: it is necessary not to abandon the passion for ultimate truth, the eagerness to search for it or the audacity to forge new paths in the search. It is faith which stirs reason to move beyond all isolation and willingly to run risks so that it may attain whatever is beautiful, good and true. Faith thus becomes the convinced and convincing advocate of reason. (no. 56)

During the Enlightenment, reason and liberty were elevated in opposition against faith and the enslavement that the Church had supposedly engineered. Meanwhile, today, it is clearly evident that the Church is the only institution in the world defending liberty and the dignity of reason against a nihilist and relativist distrust of the cognitive capacities of autonomous reason. Contemporary reason is greatly tempted to deny the plenitude of truth and, instead, to close in on itself, aiming only at fragmentary cognition. That is why faith calls upon reason to trust in the capacities that are its own, so that with its natural forces it will come to know the truth about being, the nature of things, anthropology, sexual complementarity, the principles of ethics, psychology, pedagogy, and so on.

Reason has within its structure the drive toward truth and the capacity to know this truth, even though by itself it does not reach out to the supernatural, to the mystery of faith. That is why reason has duties toward the truth, once it knows it. Maybe reason's skeptical evasion of the fullness of cognition—and its enclosure within the sphere of only opinions and conjectures, so as not to assert the truth—has its source precisely in the fact that known truth is binding, and so it generates obligations. People today do not want to know the duties that derive from truth, and so they prefer to persist in nihilism and relativism. When the Redemption and the grace that enables attachment to the truth about the good are unknown, what is left then is a paralyzing experience of moral feebleness. Thus, the escape from demanding truth and the invention of theories about the impossibility of knowing it by reason are a facile solution.

St. John Paul II did not accept such minimalism of reason, and he courageously repeated that revelation received in faith does not wound the reason, but rather it "stirs the human mind to ceaseless effort; indeed, it impels reason continually to extend the range of its knowledge,"[42] because "the coming of Christ ... redeemed reason from its weakness, setting it free from the shackles in which it had imprisoned itself."[43]

On the basis of its natural dignity, reason has the right to react to all questions, and so in its scientific inquiry it may focus in any direction whatsoever, turning also to what it finds most interesting, namely, God, but where it finds a dark, or rather blinding, spot. Since natural reason may engage in all scientific endeavors, it asks about God too. It does this within the philosophy of God (called sometimes "natural theology" or "theodicy"). Philosophical reason has the ability and the right to ponder the Absolute and the cause and end of everything that exists. In this cognition, however, reason stumbles across a frontier that it cannot transcend in spite of the development of cognitive methods used in all other sciences. Having resort only to its own methods, reason is unable to penetrate the impenetrable mystery of the living God. Reason may, with difficulty, know about God and that He exists—but as for who He is and how He enters into a relationship with us, reason alone has no inkling.

Since in God there are three Persons, it is impossible to reduce the living God to the rank of an object that is subjected to

[42] Ibid., no. 14.

[43] Ibid., no. 22.

experimental cognition, or to the level of a response to a riddle, or even to the status of an all-explaining Absolute. A person is always *a mystery* that cannot ever be exhausted. That is why the personal God hides within a mystery, which has to be received as such, and which is penetrated only through faith, which God grants as a gift to whomever He wills. In this faith there is a place for trust, and that leads to hope and to love. Paradoxically, therefore, by hiding in the mystery that is penetrated only by faith, God reveals His personal face.

Conclusions derived from philosophical reflection about God the Absolute, even though they are important and precious, are not the same as meeting the living God in faith. God above all is concerned about encountering us in a paternal-filial relationship and not just in satisfying our human curiosity. For divine grace to be set in motion within us there has to be a pure and fundamental meeting with God in faith and love. Perseverance in the relationship with God through faith is more important than the acquisition of knowledge, even philosophical knowledge about God as the Absolute. That is why contact with the living God is not to be deformed by sifting it through the sieve of considerations, ideas, and criteria that are external to faith.

The reason may engage in all sciences. But when at the same time it is open in faith to the mystery of God, it knows that in each reality studied there is an extra dimension that locates this reality in relationship to the divine paternity that *precedes the act of creation of that same reality*. This dimension pointing to the loving God cannot be known by reason alone. Faith—as it allows for an encounter with the living God, and receives the revealed and handed-down subject matter of faith on the basis of the authority of the self-disclosing God—supplies reason with a correcting perspective that extends cognition beyond the mere object of scientific inquiry. That is why theology, which is thinking within faith, is the queen of all sciences. It accepts as the point of departure the revealed truths. It does not prove them, because it does not possess tools that could do this, but rather it only looks into the revealed truths, drawing essential conclusions from them that have a bearing on the cognition of every other reality.

When God disposes the human mind through faith to receive the First Truth and to ignite grace within the soul, which is fundamental for the spiritual life, there still remains in the human mind a place for philosophical cognition based on the natural capabilities of reason. And there is also a place for theological reflection, in which reason searches for the intelligibility of the truths of faith.

In philosophy, reason, using its natural capacities, searches for the ultimate cause of everything that it knows. It can also come to know those natural truths whose subject matter corresponds with revealed truth, but which can be known by independent reason. Some truths overlap. We know them thanks to the natural effort of reason, and we *also* know them thanks to revelation. Due to the natural effort of reason we know about the existence of the human soul, which distinguishes humans from animals. We know about the natural dignity of the human being and the basic moral values. Revelation confirms these truths. Philosophy also takes up broader questions, provoking the mind to generate answers about the meaning of life and to grant a view of the whole of reality that goes beyond the fragmentary perceptions of particular sciences. And, finally, philosophy habituates the reason to be precise and exact in its reasoning and to know how to justify what it knows.

In theology the mind works toward understanding the content of faith and its internal meaning, and then it draws conclusions from this. In this effort theology uses the precise mental processes that philosophy has developed, but it always deals with the particular truths, disclosed in revelation and received by faith, that allow one to participate in the wisdom of God. Faith does not supply knowledge about astronomy, biology, or history; it speaks only about what is necessary for salvation. In faith, truths about the humanity and the divinity of the Son of God, about the Church, and about the sacraments are received, and they are believed in because one believes the First Truth, God, Who is truthful.

Positive theology, as it looks into these truths, describes how in the history of salvation, with the help of specific notions and events, God revealed Himself and entered into a relationship with people. Speculative theology, basing itself on positive theology, tries to grasp these truths exactly through precise terms that faithfully embrace the mysterious reality and facilitate the adherence of reason to it. In this cognitive effort, there is no attempt to prove the revealed truths or to test them through the natural criteria of reasoning or experimentation, because this would be something like the sin of Adam or the tactics of the philosophers of suspicion. This would lower God to the level of the human mind. The facts of the Incarnation and the Redemption are not proven, nor is the fact that human faculties receive extra gifts from God. Theology deals with God on the basis of what God has said about Himself, and it profits from the precise specification of these truths that has taken place in the history of the Church.

The cognitive effort of theology does not search for the *rationality of faith*. It only tries to bring out its *intelligibility*; that is, it tries to grasp the contours of the truth that the intellect may receive. Thanks to this, we may not only *believe* but may also know *what we believe in*, and we may know *what it means to believe*. In the light of the received teaching and experience of the great saints, we may also perceive that sometimes there is some setback in our faith, that it has not yet grown within us, and that so far it has not brought supernatural fruits in all the dimensions of life.

Since faith is located both in the intellect and, partly, in the will, belief as such is not a matter of feelings. Of course, humans are a composite whole, and so confessed and living faith has an impact on decisions that are made, and it generates an echo in the entire psyche. Emotional experiences and imaginations therefore play a role in religiosity, which expresses faith and maintains it in the personal and social realm, but the force of their expression is not a sign of the depth of faith. Some people react to everything emotionally, and so they also experience their religiosity in this way, and others are more reserved in their reactions. This does not mean that those who are cooler have no faith. In pondering about faith and its deepening, the focus should not stop short at the level of emotional experiences. It is not essential to have religious experiences, nor that they necessarily be multiplied. What is much more important is concern that faith will grow, that it will be more deeply rooted in the intellectual and moral life, thereby opening it to the fecundity of grace. This entails persistence in openness to the mystery, both the mystery expressed in the confession of faith, and also that more difficult one that unfolds itself in life.

Many people have espoused the view, maybe as a distant consequence of Luis Molina, and certainly as a result of the Enlightenment mentality, that the reason may and even should be skeptical, whereas faith has a place only on the level of feelings. In this view the intellectual life can take place only *beyond* faith. Faith then does not connect with culture or with conclusions drawn from scientific knowledge, and it does not permeate the moral life. Religious life, with its occasional moments of private and communal enthusiasm, follows one track and the intellectual and moral life—views about the world, life, economics, politics, as well as practical choices made in personal, family, professional, cultural, and social life, and also in work and in recreation—are all assessed and decided upon, on this understanding, completely outside faith.

Allowing the mystery of faith to accede to all these spheres is not easy. At the crossroads of science and faith, and of real-life decisions and faith, often the encounter is difficult. These meeting points may be a real cross. That is why life is easier when these spheres never encounter faith at all, or when their encounters are only superficial. The separation between skeptical reason and sentimental, experiential faith makes life smoother, because faith is then not treated seriously. But then this means that the vitality of grace, triggered by faith, is excluded from many walks of life. As a result, the intellectual life and personal, moral, and psychic dramas are all experienced without the support of divine grace, without remembering the words of Jesus: "Cut off from me you can do nothing" (John 15:5). Escape from the mystery of the divine life only *seemingly* facilitates earthly life. In time comes the painful experience of the insufficiency on one's own natural capabilities.

In Poland, the expression "insulting of religious feelings" is often used. It derives from communist-period jargon. This phrase was introduced by atheists, who denied faith, but in the spirit of natural moral honesty assessed making fun of religiosity as inappropriate. Undoubtedly in healthy social relationships one avoids attitudes and utterances that are irritating and insulting. Only spiteful unbelievers amuse themselves by provoking the religious sensibility of believers and then observing their reactions. The ridicule of faith is painful, but believers know that this happens in the journey of faith. Faith is often rejected by others and this is understandable, because it is a challenge for and to the autonomous reason. Some people, therefore, react to faith with indifference and others do so with scorn.

Just as "insulting religious feelings" is assessed negatively, so should one treat the more frequent "insulting of sexual feelings" that is common in advertisements, entertainment, and the media. In fact, all unwanted stimulation of the emotions from without, in particular when it is empty, is enervating, because it impedes the appropriate integration of the emotional sphere with the spiritual. Romantic literature aroused the emotions, but this was tied with moral values such as fidelity, patriotism, and generosity. When emotions are stirred in the name of *the experience itself*, so as to stimulate an adrenaline rush, whether in a sports stadium, at a rock concert, or through pornography, this is tiring and exhausting because it is washed out of values. And so, when religious emotions are aroused in the liturgy, this always has to be done in the name of faith, so as to deepen it. But if this happens within pastoral "happenings" that are poor in the transmission of the content of faith and in which the actual prayerful expression of faith is hardly present, the fruitfulness of such stimulations is meager.

In response to the expression "insulting religious feelings" one needs to insist that faith in principle is not a matter of feelings, even religious feelings. Rather, it concerns convictions, and decisions made on the basis of these convictions. Religious freedom is manifested by the fact that one has not only the right to experience religious emotions and not have them wounded, but, much more importantly, one has the right to have convictions flowing from faith and the right to engage in actions in private and public life that are based upon them.

Above all, it must always be remembered that faith is important primarily because it triggers the life of grace. The expression of faith within every human situation opens the soul to divine power, without which "we can do nothing"—or, rather, we can do something, but ultimately that action turns out to be futile, irrelevant, and deprived of the divine support that God wants to grant and that passes through human hands, hearts, and minds. A true witness to the faith does not just defend religious moods, which may be variable, but defends the confession of faith, its recognition as being true, and its engagement in actions.

The role of apologetics

Faith does not question the dignity of reason, but the reception of faith is not the end point of purely rational thinking. In faith there is assent to the truth, not because in itself it is conclusively evident, but because the authority of a witness has been recognized. And that witness is God Himself. This is why it is impossible to induce anybody to belief through rational argumentation. In faith, in addition to the functioning of reason, there is also the input of the will. No one believes without wanting to do so. The role of the will in faith extends beyond stimulating the intellect so that it accepts the revealed, often nebulous, truth. The will also supplies the motive of faith. The believer believes, because, due to a movement of internal grace, he recognizes that God has revealed truths, and he trusts Him.

Just as faith is not a conclusion derived from reasoning alone, so also it is not solely an act of the will desiring to believe, even against reason. A fideist approach, in which reason claims one thing and a trustful will declares itself in favor of something contrary, with both stands accepted simultaneously, knowing that this is absurd, is unacceptable. If a man of science rationally accepts as true only some residual information about the historical Jesus or even doubts about His factual existence and, at the same time, recognizes the Christ of faith, he persists in an attitude that is schizophrenic. Since faith does not exclude reason, faith cannot be an irrational assent of the will that allows for the absurd. In faith, there is a place for the examination of its reasoned credibility.

Credibility refers to the quality of the witness—that is, the recognition that the witness is worthy of trust. Also in natural faith there is such an assessment of the credibility of the witness. We can have confidence in a friend who informed us about the scheduled departure of a train and, at the same time, we may check the timetable. This is not necessarily a lack of trust in the friend, but a reaching out to a more dependable witness. In faith that is received from God as a grace, there is also a place for external testimonies and witnesses of faith who lead one toward God. To truly believe, we have to know *that we need to believe* and *that there is a basis for faith.*[44] This basis is something other than seeing directly the truth in which one believes.

The argument in favor of belief is not an objective proof of the truth. Its function consists in maintaining the mind in belief. But we are bound by the morality of the intellect: We do not believe in fancies and just anybody who happens to demand belief. We do not suspend our entire life on the words of some chance witness. And so we need to check whether the testimony of the witness is justified and whether belief in matters to which the witness is pointing is really appropriate. Faith needs a moral certitude, which is not the same as scientific certitude; it is too serious an issue to depend on conjectures or wishful thinking. What is at stake is credibility. It has to be ascertained whether belief is necessary, and whether the proposed truths have been indicated by an authorized witness. It is not a question of searching for arguments that will convincingly embrace the truth itself. Faith is never the fruit of proof, scientific or other. It is, and remains, faith.

Rational arguments confirming the truths of faith, references to the Scriptures, doctrinal teaching from the *Catechism*, pointing out the nonhuman origin of the Church as reflected in Her vitality, the witness of charismatic graces and inexplicable miracles, or the appeal to the authority of serious people who believe: All these may support the idea that belief is justified. But they do not supply faith

[44] *Summa Theologiae*, Ia-IIae, q. 1, art. 4, ad. 2: *Non enim crederet nisi videret ea esse credenda, vel propter evidentiam signorum, vel propter aliquid huiusmodi.*

itself, which remains the adherence to God in view of Him alone. They only manifest that faith is not absurd—that it is credible.

In respect to faith itself, these multiple reasons of credibility are secondary: They only *confirm* that in faith God is really drawing us to Himself. They can be compared to a regal seal on a document confirming that the king has truly spoken, but which has no influence on the subject matter of the document. Reasons that point to the credibility of faith can sway the will, but they have no influence on the object of faith. Ultimately it is not so important how they spur the will from without. Some people are moved by extraordinary events that draw them to faith. Others are more moved by the authority of respected individuals. And there are others who view everything in a catastrophic way, and so in the movement of their will toward faith, their fear plays a major role. And yet others are supported by rational arguments or personal experiences. These reasons of credibility influence the will from without in various ways, but they all confirm that belief in view of God is appropriate.

It is the task of apologetics to produce such arguments and to provoke an initial recognition that faith is not absurd, but sensible. Apologetics are not scientific proofs that justify the content of faith. When there were attempts in apologetics to present such scientific proofs, they elicited understandable resistance because this bordered on intellectual manipulation. Scientific conclusions are not to be manipulated to fit faith. So, too, the supernatural motive of faith is not to be lowered to purely human reasons. The adherence to revealed truth in view of God within faith, which is a grace, is one thing, and knowing reasons showing that that credence is not absurd is another.

Carefully delineating between the two extremities of fideism and rationalism, Vatican Council I on the one hand stressed the supernatural character of faith—its derivation from grace such that "we believe that what [God] has revealed is true, not because the intrinsic truth of things is recognized by the natural light of reason, but because of the authority of God Himself who reveals them"[45]—and, on the other hand, declared that "God willed that exterior proofs of His revelation, viz., divine facts, especially miracles and prophecies, should be joined to the interior helps of the Holy Spirit."[46] The council did not settle the issue of whether these external arguments necessarily have to be supported by the movement of the Holy Spirit so as to become convincing. The council listed among these external reasons the miracles and prophecies known from the Scriptures and also pointed to the Church:

> The Church by herself, with her marvelous propagation, eminent holiness and inexhaustible fruitfulness in everything that is good, with her Catholic unity and invincible stability, is a great and perpetual motive of credibility and an irrefutable testimony of her divine mission.[47]

We might wonder whether basing the credibility of faith on the attentive study of the Church is not somewhat excessive or even naïve. The council presumed here that the historical observation of the Church leads to the conviction that it is some moral and sociological miracle. Which other social institution can boast of such a distant genealogy, such durability and capacity for permanent renewal? But this argument does not speak convincingly to all. It has to be remembered, however, that this evidence was cited not as a *proof* that justifies faith, which would be a denial of faith and its replacement by knowledge, but as an *argument that authenticates credence.* It demonstrates that faith in God is not absurd.

[45] *The Christian Faith in the Doctrinal Documents*, no. 118.

[46] Ibid., no. 119.

[47] Ibid., no. 123.

The council did not insist that all be moved by such arguments. Some may be more inclined to faith by the fact that it concords with some subjective experience or psychic need. Thus, in the recognition of the reliability of signs and evidences that speak in favor of faith, personal factors and dispositions play a major role. But assurance is needed to avoid personal illusions or subjection to some external manipulation. That is why there is a place in faith for ascertaining evidence of credibility, but as the believer grows in faith, these apologetic arguments become less important. What then becomes more important for the believer is that his faith grows nourished by itself, that is, by the encounter with God through grace. Thus, it is necessary to move beyond the level of apologetics and beyond analyzing arguments that support the credibility of faith.

Faith and the philosophy of God

Supernatural faith is the entry of God, the First Truth, into the activity of the mind—that is, the adapting of the mind by divine power so that an encounter with God and openness to His action become possible. How then does faith differ from a natural search for truth, even the highest truth? By its natural functioning endowed by the Creator, and not as a result of a special gift of grace, human reason *can* know the truth. On the basis of this natural capacity and curiosity, human reason can raise every imaginable question within philosophy, and so it can formulate anthropological questions about the specificity of humanness, the relationship of the body to the soul, and life and death; ethical questions about the essence of goodness and evil and the meaning of love and suffering; cosmological questions about the world, time, and space; and also metaphysical questions about the first cause and end of being—that is, ultimately about God. In an honest, rigorously correct thinking within philosophy, the reason can find true answers to these questions.

It would be erroneous to judge faith as completely indifferent to such natural enquiries. Faith does not demand a weak mind. A strong mind, practiced in the search for truth about everything that exists, is valued by faith—on the condition that it does not claim the right to deny faith or to subordinate it to its own criteria. Since the world and natural reason that studies it derive from the Creator, there can be no essential contradiction between truth that has been acquired through the natural cognitive capacities of reason and faith that is received from the Savior, the Giver of grace. Faith, therefore, is not afraid of reason, and in no way does the believer escape from truth, because he knows that every truth has its ultimate source in God. This does not, of course, mean that the development of a strong reason in itself is sufficient for salvation, or that reason may set itself up as a barrier against faith, excluding or despising it. It should not be surprising that the life of faith and the opening to grace in all dimensions of life does not necessarily go hand in hand with a developed intellectual life. Sometimes simple, uncomplicated people with a childlike faith advance more deeply in the spiritual life than those who stop short, on the level of the *ratio*, taking more delight in the achievements of their reason.

A fully justified, purely natural search for truth about the Absolute that explains all and is the ultimate cause and end of all being pertains to the philosophy of God. This natural philosophical discipline, sometimes called "theodicy," differs from theology, which in faith receives truths that have been revealed, and then looks into them. In England the "philosophy of God" or "theodicy" is called "natural theology." This term is somewhat misleading, because it obscures the fact that this discourse is purely rational, based only on what the reason may know and justify about God by its own efforts, and so this is not a *theological* discourse. Even more so, the recently coined expression "philosophical theology" is confusing and internally contradictory. It dangerously approaches the mumbo-jumbo mixing of philosophy with theology, that is, of reason with faith. When a philosophical discourse undertakes specifically theological themes, to which reason itself has no access, this leaves the impression that the truths of faith are being presented, when in fact what is presented is an external description of a sociological or phenomenological nature, without penetrating the mysterious contents of faith, by faith. This inquiry might incline the mind to reflect upon some statement of faith, and eventually even to accept it, but only if it appears to be convincing, purely out of a rational motivation, and not because the truth has been revealed and presented as a belief by the Church.

One needs therefore to check carefully whether discourses that present themselves as "natural theology" or "philosophical theology" are nothing more than a philosophy of the Absolute, or, worse, whether they have slipped into Gnosticism by mixing faith with science—in other words, transforming faith into knowledge, thereby subordinating revealed faith to natural reasons and criteria. It is worth recalling here that St. Thomas Aquinas clearly distinguished the philosophical discourse from the theological. His *Summa Contra Gentiles*, a fundamental work planned as an exposition of Christian wisdom in confrontation with the positions of infidels, was divided according to what reason alone may know of the truth (books 1–3) and what reason may know uniquely thanks to the reception of revelation by faith (book 4). Aquinas obviously distinguished the philosophical discourse from the theological and did not mix them.

A purely philosophical reflection that abstracts from faith or goes completely beyond it, studying the nature of the human mind and its way of functioning, perceives in the mind a natural desire to see God. The human reason may, on the basis of its own effort, arrive at the conclusion that God exists and that had He not existed, the existence of all reality would be absurd. The possibility of knowing the truth about the existence of God through natural, rational reflection beginning with an observation of existing reality has been confirmed by Vatican Council I[48]—even though, of course, arriving at the truth about God's existence by reason alone is by no means easy. Not all people arrive at such a conclusion directly, and those who do often mix known truth with error.

Since the existence of God may be known through natural effort, curiosity about this God appears in the reason. And so, in the structure of the mind, there is a natural desire, or rather, speaking precisely, a natural tendency toward seeing God as the source and end of everything that exists. This natural desire to see God is not innate; it springs from curiosity, generated in the mind after having arrived at the truth that God exists.

The claim that the desire for the vision of God appears in *the structure* of the mind is not a conclusion derived from observation of religiosity among men, and so it is not a result of studies in ethnography or psychology, even though such observations *confirm* the curiosity of the mind reaching out toward questions about God. The natural desire for the vision of God derives *directly* from the structure of the intellect; the human mind, in its openness to the universal, has within itself the tendency to search for truth, including the ultimate truth. Once the mind arrives at the conclusion that God exists, there arises a curiosity about that God, and the mind wants to know more about Him. But in this inquiry the mind comes across a blinding light, and so ultimately there is little that it can know about God through its natural effort. It remains

[48] Ibid., no. 115.

in the darkness that results from the inability of the natural mind to grasp the fullness of God. But this does not weaken the curiosity present within the mind and the possibility of cognition. And so, sometimes, when the attainment of the object of this natural desire becomes difficult, the discouraged individual pushes it aside or reacts like the fox in the ancient fable, who, when he noticed that the grapes were too high, went away sad, telling himself that they were probably sour anyway.

The philosophical cognitive effort that strives to grasp some knowable contours of the reality that is the ultimate Absolute is valid. It expresses the most basic scientific cognition. Incidentally, it also shows that the eternal life promised in revelation, consisting in the knowing of God (John 17:3), does not promise a deformation of the mind. Instead, it corresponds to the natural, most noble inclinations of the human spirit. But the acquired, yet natural, desire to see God, and the *philosophy* of God that ensues, is not the fruit of supernatural grace but, rather, an expression of natural curiosity. This does not entail a real union with the personal God made possible by faith, together with the other theological virtues. The philosophy of God is a sign of an intriguing search for knowledge that reaches out to the maximally attainable fruit of the natural effort of the human mind. It points to the dignity of that mind, one that does not lock itself within self-imposed reductionist limits. Philosophical inquiry is proof that the most ultimate questions are not extraneous to man and that human reason is capable of engaging with them, even if the results of these difficult pursuits are meager. It is not surprising, therefore, that probing such questions in a scientific, exact manner that can be logically explained and justified is something that only exceptional individuals can do, even though many people in various moments of life express some natural curiosity about God in a less reflective manner.

We have therefore two orders of cognition: One that is supernatural, stemming from the gift of faith, and the other that is natural, that is, philosophical. The first, deriving from divine grace, does not require any special intellectual capacities, even though it does not deny them and can coexist with them. The other is essentially a manifestation of the philosophizing mind, which means that it is more elitist. The Church insists upon this distinction and requires that these two orders should not be intermingled, so that faith will not be subordinated to natural cognition.[49] In so doing the Church rejects the Protestant distrust of reason and the idea that reason must capitulate to faith in order for faith to be welcomed in the soul.

Philosophical inquiry about God is a supreme manifestation of natural intellectual work, and so it deserves respect—but it is not identical to faith. In philosophical cognition, reason employs its own power and methods so as to scrape out of reality known truths. Reason then tries to articulate these truths through notions and concepts that it had worked out. Meanwhile, the living God is greater than knowledge seized by reason or even the end result of the curiosity of philosophers. God is a living, personal God, Who yearns for encounter with His children. That is why God grants the gift of faith, a supernatural adapting of the human mind so that it accepts the First Truth that is God. Furthermore, God has expressed the content of faith through historical revelation, and these truths are then handed down to the faithful by the Church. In His grace God also grants the remaining theological virtues, and through them an interpersonal union of God with humans and humans with God comes about.

In philosophical cognition there is some, even if only fractional, dominion over the known object, something that cannot exist

[49] *The Christian Faith in the Doctrinal Documents*, no. 131.

in a real interpersonal relationship. By contrast, in supernatural faith there is the *humility* of the intellect, which faces a reality that transcends it and receives the truths of faith as a gift. Furthermore, there is openness to the supernatural life of grace, which is set in motion by that living faith.

Since faith is a divine gift, there is no such thing as a natural desire of the supernatural.[50] Such a wording, which incidentally is internally contradictory, suggests that the hunger of the supernatural derives from a purely natural human investigation, or that as a result, and on the basis of a natural search, there comes about a spontaneous leap into the supernatural order. Such an interpretation is contrary to the Church's teaching, which has been articulated since antiquity. The yearning for God, even if it expresses some initial and very feeble, yet real, encounter with God, is already a consequence of grace.[51]

The famous utterance of St. Augustine about the disquiet in the human heart until it rests in God was written within a prayerful confession addressed to God. It does not, therefore, describe a purely rational philosophical discourse that nature itself is capable of without grace. Of course, it is difficult to ascertain with scientific exactitude whether somebody is acting solely due to nature, or whether the individual is internally moved by grace, since grace cannot be felt. Many natural searches of the Absolute may be moved mysteriously from within by divine grace. In fact, most philosophers engaged in reflecting about God are already

[50] Cardinal H. de Lubac, who has great merit in raising the issue of the relationship of nature to the supernatural in Catholic theology of the twentieth century, erroneously suggested that a natural desire of grace is possible.

[51] Cf. Canon 6 of the Second Council of Orange (529) quoted above in the section on the genesis of faith.

believers as they look into natural reasons that lead the mind to the truth of the existence of God.

The claim that it is possible to move naturally from the philosophy of God to a faith that enables an "encounter" with God[52] gives rise to far-reaching erroneous consequences. Those who begin with a rational analysis or a philosophical, sociological, or psychological description of some reality and then suddenly leap into a theological discourse of faith may think they are doing a service to faith. This, however, is an ill turn. Either it points to the proper dignity of rational discourse, but erroneously assesses supernatural faith by naïvely viewing it as something that can be logically deduced from rational discourse, and, perhaps, even reducing that faith to the rank of a purely natural trust untethered from God. Or this flawed claim, that it is possible to move naturally from the philosophy of God to supernatural faith, reflects the insufficiency and limitations of one's rational arguments, and so, precisely for this reason, one reaches out to revealed truths. These flawed ways of thinking generate the impression that faith is a logical consequence of knowledge, or even that faith serves above all, and even uniquely, to fill in the gaps of a particular rational discourse. Faith then is turned into a resource for the deficiencies of scientific cognition, which then generates the hope that as scientific cognition develops, there will be fewer gaps that need to be filled in by faith. Such a train of thought, if it is undertaken by somebody who is positively disposed to Christianity, expresses a hidden presupposition that the need for

[52] The Second Council of Orange insisted that faith has to be "as is required"—*sicut oportet*. The Council of Trent repeated this phrase (*The Christian Faith in the Doctrinal Documents*, no. 1953), and Vatican Council I stressed the importance of the distinction between divine faith and a natural knowledge of God (*The Christian Faith in the Doctrinal Documents*, no. 126).

faith will come about on its own, naturally, from the conclusions of the stimulated mind.

This is completely contrary to the experience of St. Paul. He never searched for Christ and did not come across Him as a result of philosophical inquiries or due to his discouragement with the weakness of natural reasoning and natural ethics. St. Paul met Jesus, not through his own initiative, but through His. The expectation that faith is born directly from the queries and searches of autonomous reason are naïve and contrary to the experience of faith. The presentation of an extensive scientific discourse on a purely rational level beyond faith, as if the living, self-revealing God did not exist, *sicut Deus non esset*, by no means leads to faith, nor does it deepen it.

The suggestion that faith is born of natural philosophical reflection is the heart of Semi-Pelagianism. This heresy accepts the need of faith and grace, but it claims that the first moment of belief is the result of a purely natural search. Holding this erroneous view blocks the divine life. What is missing here are the recognition of the primacy of divine action within the soul and a wondrous gratitude for the already present grace of faith. When this erroneous reasoning is applied to oneself, or to others, there is a continuous retreat from the order of faith and a transfer to the level of rational discourse, which presumably may lead to faith in the future.

But, in fact, he who already believes even feebly and sluggishly—if he desires God and attempts to move toward Him despite not knowing how to do this, and if he occasionally prays, watches, tries, pleads, searches, or knocks, despite the fact that these moments of focusing on God are interrupted and seemingly ineffective—has already been touched by God and has already been gifted with the supernatural life. It is not necessary, therefore, to push oneself or others out from the spiritual life by transferring to the level of purely rational discourse. What is needed is belief in the existence of the supernatural spiritual life, belief that even this anemic faith ensures a contact with God. Maybe initially the contact is minute, but with an appropriate nourishing this nascent faith will grow and enliven the entire soul from within. The spiritual life of believers consists in the development of the grace of faith that was received at Baptism, even if the opening up to that grace and its admittance to all dimensions of life is a slow process that requires prayer and gradual purification.

The natural philosophizing reason can know only the general contours of God without penetrating the interior of His mystery. Only faith can reach out further than this general picture, touching the living God directly. And only faith ignites the supernatural life in the soul, so that it moves the person from within. Faith is a manifestation of the working of divine grace and, as such, it does not require some high intellectual level and philosophical knowledge. Small children are capable of maintaining a real spiritual bond with God through faith. This faith is always supernatural, even though its rooting in the soul and its impact on life may be varied. Faith may grow and it may wane, and so in different people and in varying moments of life it does not manifest itself in the same way. It should not therefore be expelled from the psyche by an autonomous reason that defends its independence from faith and rejects the idea that an encounter with God requires the attribution of primacy to God and not to oneself.

The study of the philosophy of God, philosophy of religion, ethnography, and history is fully justified and permissible, but this cognitive effort is not to be mistaken for faith. One should not expect a deepening of faith resulting from such scientific research. Faith is a supernatural reality that initiates the movement of divine life within the soul. Its development needs appropriate foods that are different than philosophical enquiries.

A philosophical toying with faith

How then are we to assess the thesis that one should temporarily suspend faith so as to subject it to methodological suspicion, during which the objective reasons justifying the credibility of its content are checked and then, upon resolution of difficulties, one returns to faith based now on a more solid, rational basis? Such an intellectual procedure was proposed in the nineteenth century by Georg Hermes, who was influenced by the philosophy of Kant. He postulated the conscious reception of a real and not only fictitious doubt concerning the faith, so as to prove on the basis of criteria that are external to faith that enlightened minds may accept it. Hermes distinguished between a reasonable faith and that of the heart. The first, preferred by him, does not need grace and is based on the unaided philosophizing reason, and the other, in accord with Church doctrine, may grow out of grace.[53] This represented the classical linkage of reason with skepticism, and it treated the faith of the uneducated as a purely sentimental phenomenon. Grace within faith was regarded as inessential—not worthy of the serious man's attention. The position of Hermes was condemned by Pope Gregory XVI.[54]

Vatican Council I, perhaps reacting to Hermes's thesis, rejected the claim that "assent to the Christian faith ... is produced with necessity by arguments of human reason,"[55] and that

> Catholics could have a just reason for suspending their judgment and calling into question the faith that they have already received under the teaching authority of the Church,

[53] Dulles, *The Assurance of Things Hoped For*, pp. 81–82, 252.

[54] H. Denzinger and A. Schönmetzer, *Enchiridion Symbolorum, Definitionum et Declarationum de Rebus Fide et Morum* (Barcinonae, Friburgi Brisgoviae, Romae: Herder, 1975), no. 2739.

[55] *The Christian Faith in the Doctrinal Documents*, no. 129.

until they have completed a scientific demonstration of the credibility and truth of their faith.[56]

The reason the council rejected such philosophical tinkering with faith is obvious. He who brackets his faith instead of confessing it, and tries to analyze its contents and to justify it by arguments based solely on reason, suggesting that faith merits serious treatment only when it fits his reasoning, kills the faith that is in him. The exclusion of the supernatural motive of faith places oneself and one's subjective reasons above the revealing God and abolishes the disposition to divine grace that needs to be continuously maintained by faith. "Whoever remains in me, with me in him, bears fruit in plenty; for cut off from me you can do nothing. Anyone who does not remain in me is like a branch that has been thrown away—he withers" (John 15:5–6).

Such games that elevate one's own intellectual sharpness above a faith received on the authority of the self-revealing God are lethal to the spiritual life, even if faith still lingers somehow in the extra-intellectual, traditional-sentimental sphere of the psyche. This means that the encounter with God, and persevering in Him, is excluded from the intellectual and moral life, appearing only in inessential, occasional moments that touch the heart. It is not surprising then that attempts to sort out the moral life based only on philosophically worked-out ethical reasons, without an initiation into the mysterious divine grace, are doomed to failure. Moreover, the reduction of faith to the realm of emotional experiences—even intensive, communal ones that are sometimes coupled with patriotic events—is often on par with a practical life played out completely beyond faith, outside of openness to grace and blind to the guidance of the Gospel.

[56] *The Christian Faith in the Doctrinal Documents*, no. 130.

It should not be claimed that the assessment of faith from the height of a purely intellectual judgment free of faith was only a temptation of proud ancient Gnostics, who were hammered by St. Irenaeus of Lyon, or of the post-Enlightenment atmosphere of the nineteenth century. This view is also currently enticing.

A purely rational reflection on the content of faith, describing itself as "philosophical theology," has to be seen as what it is: the destruction of faith. It begins from the start with the rejection of supernatural revelation and accuses theology of persisting in an "extrarational space" identified with superstition.

Theology has to respect the research of the philosophy of God, which considers the Absolute and its necessary attributes by reason alone, but it also has the right to expect a similar esteem coming from philosophy. Philosophy has no tools to deal with the truths of faith that are known uniquely due to revelation. If it wonders whether the Blessed Trinity can be "demonstrated," or if it directly claims that it has worked out a philosophical proof of the necessity of the Incarnation or has rationally explained the essence of the eternal life in God, it has gone beyond its field of vision.[57] All this

[57] An example of such a basically Gnostic discourse can be found in the work of S. Judycki, *Bóg i inne osoby. Próba z zakresu teologii filozoficznej* (God and other persons: an attempt in the field of philosophical theology) (Poznań: W drodze, 2010), which is the first of the series of Open Lectures in Natural Theology in the Honor of J.M. Bocheński, OP. Judycki wants to "justify the basic truths of faith in such a way that they can be called knowledge," and this is to be done on the basis of "arguments that are outside of Revelation" (p. 30). He proposes a "specific type of philosophical argumentation about the truth of the Trinitarian dogma" (p. 73) and claims on the basis of his reasoning that "the Incarnation was necessary" (p. 75). He treats the faith of believers as a sort of "inexplicable intuition," comparable to dogs' sense of smell (p. 103)! Judycki is not interested in the spiritual life. He does not admit an actual encounter with God initiated by faith, about which Aquinas says that it is an

may be viewed as a methodological error and an excessive fancy of reason. Care is needed, however, to ensure that such discourses are kept distant from faith and not mixed with theology. They cannot be called theology, either natural or philosophical. This is because they suggest that theology is based upon purely rational investigations and that they play some essential role in the life of faith.

Those who are fascinated by their own intellectual capacities may be impressed by such considerations, but they may fail to notice the intellectual pride into which they have fallen. Their reception of the truths of faith is subordinated to philosophical reasons, often debatable and doubtful, and not based upon the authority of the self-revealing God and the Church that transmits them. This does not lead to growth in the spiritual life. Furthermore, when at some future moment it is discovered that the proposed philosophical arguments are not convincing, the rejection of faith ensues.

Such a discourse, which does not directly deny the truths of faith but, instead, supposedly justifies them by its arguments, appears on the surface to be kindly disposed toward the faith. In reality, its apparent sympathy destroys the decisive motive of faith and so cuts it down.

Purely philosophical reflections on the scenes from the Gospels undertaken consciously outside faith should be judged in a similar way.[58] Treating the Gospels solely as a description of people and

inchoatio vitae aeternae, whereas he extensively speculates about the philosophical illumination of eternal life after death (p. 142) and claims that he possesses "the means for a speculative reconstruction of transfigured consciousness" (p. 159).

[58] An example of such considerations is the work of M. Grabowski, *Pomazaniec. Przyczynek do chrystologii filozoficznej* (The anointed: a contribution to philosophical Christology) (Poznań: W drodze, 2011), the second piece in the series of Open Lectures in Natural Theology in the Honor of J.M. Bocheński, OP. Grabowski is interested in faith uniquely as "the object of … philosophical

their relationships may offer some material for philosophical anthropological consideration. Such a study, done intelligently, comparable to the literary analysis of the characters in a Shakespearean play, does allow for some perhaps illuminating insights into human attitudes, questions, wonders, reactions, and experiences of self-consciousness. Also, a purely psychological, psychoanalytical, political, Marxist, revolutionary, historical, sociological, or cultural reading of the Gospel may facilitate drawing attention to some aspects that are interesting for some. But this purely rational reflection on an evangelical text is no *lectio divina*. It does not nourish faith, nor does it deepen it. It is a clear sign that the confession of faith has been shelved. Only those who have succumbed to the heresy of Semi-Pelagianism, who are unaware that faith is a gift of grace and who treat it only as one of numerous phenomena of self-consciousness, studied by epistemology or some other science, will

inspection" (p. 10), and so faith is seen from without and not from within—though he does finally accept the necessity of faith in Jesus as a silently presumed thesis that is never directly stated in his lectures (p. 257). In his conscious methodological reduction, however, while he does not question the theological truth about the necessity of the grace of faith in Jesus, the Son of God, he locates it in a parenthesis (pp. 80–81). As a result, Grabowski easily succumbs to a note of ridicule and readily reduces faith to superstition. He finds it surprising that in the light of the Gospel "faith may be totally eccentric, so long as it is faith in Jesus" (p. 167), and that "among Christians admittedly even today there are those who choose Jesus as their Lord and give Him the right to impose tasks upon them ... but after all they do this freely" (p. 184). Being aware that he is moving away from the Chalcedonian dogma, Grabowski perceives in Jesus only a man and attributes to Him a merely human faith in place of the Beatific Vision (p. 119). Grabowski is fully conscious that he is not describing a faith that is a gift of grace, but only the "acquisition of faith," and he is analyzing the "initial steps of that process" (p. 258).

allow themselves to be talked into the erroneous view that such a discourse may serve the faith that is confessed by the Church.

It has to be remembered that the theological virtue of faith differs completely from natural, rational cognition, and from natural faith. There is, of course, a natural faith and natural trust: We do not live on the level of absolute empiricism or strict logic. We trust people and situations. We are not constantly checking everything experimentally. We trust that the train will come and hopefully on time. Trusting is a human attitude, and an expression of how we function in the world. Natural faith as an epistemological phenomenon sheds some light on our understanding of human nature, and so it may be the subject matter of precise scientific, psychological, or philosophical observation. Such analyses of natural faith are fully justified and have their place among the studies of various sciences.

But theological faith is completely different. It is a supernatural reality, a gift of grace that enables reason to receive the revealed God, the First Truth, and sets the spiritual life of the soul in motion. Faith is the first of the theological virtues infused by God in the soul. It is followed by supernatural hope and charity. Together they allow for a friendly relationship with God.

There is some similarity between natural, rational cognition and natural faith, on the one hand, and theological faith on the other, but the differences between them are even greater. Theological faith, in essence, is unique and special, because it is not a natural but, rather, a supernatural gift of God, given according to the measure of His generosity. That is why an unbeliever, either one who has not received the gift of faith or one who has received it, but then poisoned it or failed to develop it, finds theological faith inconceivable. This is because its basic orientation is not from below to above, as in scientific cognition and natural religiosity, but the exact opposite, from above to below. It is God Who leans down toward His children and endows them with His gifts, infused into the human soul so that it may engage in a friendly relationship with Him and open up to His power. "No one can come to Me unless he is drawn by the Father who sent Me" (John 6:44).

5

Growth in Faith

The life of faith

The supernatural life is a real life. It can be compared to the natural physiological, emotional, or intellectual life, even though it essentially differs from them. God grants His grace, due to which union with Him—expressing faith, trust, and friendship—is possible, and then that bond may be extended onto others. The spiritual life played out in a soul that relies on God is a true life: It may therefore grow, and it also may wane and wither. As in all life, it needs nourishment. We should not conclude that it is flimsy, just because it is frequently in tatters. The spiritual life has its own force and specific resilience against external attacks. It often happens that one is under the forceful pressure of stimuli that question faith. They may come from social influences that reject faith or ridicule it. They may also flow from the person's interiority, from an emotional involvement that engages the psyche, or from intellectual difficulties; they may be the result of the accumulation of sins, sometimes addictive ones. They may also be born from a real experience of suffering. And yet, despite all these differing adversities, which seem to expel the spiritual life completely, faith sometimes still lingers and may develop wondrously in a given moment, rebuilding the living encounter with God anew.

The spiritual life is a delicate plant, but of great vitality. It needs to be nurtured, remembering at the same time that it is a *supernatural* life, and so one that draws its force from God. The laws of development of this life differ completely from those of the bodily, emotional, or intellectual life. Sometimes in a moment of great poverty, psychic sickness, human rejection, physical suffering, or the approaching final agony, the supernatural life flourishes and enables an encounter with God, a pure and trustful abandonment to Him alone, for Him alone.

Faith sets the supernatural life in motion. Faith itself is a gift of grace, but perseverance in it—the eliciting of acts of faith, the calling in of divine support—happens through conscious action. The first impulse of the soul that enables faith is a pure divine gift, one that is completely unmerited. But once faith is given, the supernatural life is initiated, and so the subsequent steps in faith are a prodding of this life to motion. That is why the eliciting of acts of faith, growing in it, nurturing it, and learning the practice of basing oneself upon God and of allowing Him entry into one's life so as to do everything in unison with Him—and so concern that faith and supernatural charity not only will not die out, but that they will expand and become strong—requires vigilant consideration. But since the supernatural life is a real life, it possesses within itself the dynamics of its own growth.

The nourishing of faith is not like pouring fuel into a car, but like feeding an organism. The car will not move on its own without gasoline, whereas an organism may continue to live for some time without food, and it may revive after a phase of starvation. Thus, even after a period when it seemed that faith was completely dead, it may come back to life and manifest an extraordinary vitality.

Growth in faith is not to be identified with the accumulation of religious knowledge. Correct information about religion is useful, because it directs faith, focusing it toward the divine mystery, and it shows how one can live based on divine support. But religious expertise itself is not yet faith. Somebody may have extensive, absolutely correct religious knowledge, but this does not necessarily mean that he or she has faith. And true faith may be found in someone with very meager and, even on some points, erroneous religious formation. A limited knowledge of religious facts may coexist with a real trust in God, an encounter that searches for His support and counts on Him. All this may be as if groping in the dark without the backing and elucidation of religious teaching, without a precise understanding of basic catechetical or theological truths that articulate the supernatural life. Another individual may possess competent theological expertise, but in the practice of life, in particular when difficulties abound, may fail to search for God, not count on Him, or even reject Him with indignation.

Since a living faith differs from religious knowledge, it follows that the transmission of such knowledge is not to be mistaken for the maintenance and expansion of the life of faith. It is possible, therefore, and even necessary, to reflect upon the spiritual life in the soul, the principles of its growth and enlargement, the ways of nourishing and purifying it, independently from reflecting on the ways information about religious truths will be transmitted. It would be helpful here to look to the Church's accumulated wisdom expressed in Her doctrine, the experience of the saints, and theological reflection. When catechetical formation programs are prepared for children or adults, above all it has to be ensured that there is primacy of concern for the living faith. A prayerful environment is generally more conducive to growth in faith than a purely school setting. Faith is augmented by prayer, by living through faith, and not only through lectures and theological readings, even though the study of theology that describes the life of faith is obviously beneficial. This is because structured thinking that is open to the revealed mystery enables one to know better what one believes in and how, and so it becomes clear that concern for the quality of one's faith is necessary.

Faith that is infused in the soul by God is not just a single impulse, one act of faith. When God grants the grace of faith, He deposits the virtue of faith within the faculties of the soul. A virtue is a permanent disposition that allows for an almost spontaneous, easy, and creative undertaking of appropriate acts. Thus, the virtue of faith enables a regular appeal to God and openness to His power. Once the virtue of faith is already there, the extension of thinking that opens the mind to the revealed truth, in view of God, Who does not lie, becomes possible.

Repeated acts of faith awaken the virtues of hope and charity that also are of divine origin and have God as their object. As a consequence of activated faith, in hope there is reliance on God while the future unfolds, and in charity the power of God's love is brought to bear, particularly in moments when human love turns out to be weak and needs internal supernatural reinforcement. Then, on the basis of this divine support, it is possible to love courageously and with tenacity, even in the face of adversity—and what's more, enemies may even be loved. The encounter with God that is the supernatural life of the soul takes place through these three theological virtues. But it is *set in motion* by acts of the first virtue, namely, faith. Because a virtue is a permanent disposition, frequent and regular repetition of its acts is possible.

Furthermore, because faith is a virtue, it may grow. God infuses virtues at an embryonic stage, but their expansion depends upon human activity. This is the case with both the theological virtues and the moral ones that are infused with grace. Growth of knowledge consists in knowing more and with greater certitude. The growth of a virtue results in its being rooted more deeply in the soul, meaning that it triggers appropriate action with greater spontaneity and appealing creativity. Thus, since faith is a virtue, it is possible to ensure that it entails not only the adherence to a more extensive knowledge of revealed truths but also, and above all, that it truly influences daily life. When engaging faith by referring to God becomes a common and frequent reaction in various situations, great or minute, our actions are then tied with divine power. One cannot, therefore, just be satisfied that one has faith, and then ignore it. We receive faith from God so that *we will use it*. Faith has to be expressed above all internally. In this way our disposition toward divine grace expands. But also faith has to be expressed in external public confession.

When referring to God at multiple moments of the day has become a practical reflex, in work and rest, in difficulties and everyday tasks, and also during meetings with others, then faith becomes the fundamental axis of life, ensuring the constant introduction of grace into those issues that one deals with. The psyche, of course, cannot be continuously and uniquely focused upon God. This is neither possible nor necessary. It is enough that there is the general attitude, but one that is regularly repeated, at least during daily morning prayer, in which one calls God in and commits the tasks of the day to Him. Then the expressed faith ensures the openness of the soul toward God. But the more one calls upon God during the day, with momentary reflexes of faith, the more current events are permeated by His power, and so they profit from the fecundity of God Himself.

In the life of faith, three stages or, rather, moments of faith can be distinguished. At the first level, faith expresses *credo Deum esse*, that is, the declaration of the mind under the influence of the will recognizing the existence of God. This is a basic moment that comes from the impulse of grace. It differs from philosophical knowledge insisting that the existing cosmos logically must have some ultimate cause, some final end. Faith in the existence of God is a faith provoked by grace in which the truth of the existence of God is received on the basis of the authority of God Himself. God has disclosed Himself in revelation and touches the soul from within, so that it believes in His existence. This mere declaration in faith that God exists is only the first moment of the spiritual life. The next level of faith is important and expresses something more, *credo Deo,* namely, trust in God.

On the first level there is only the recognition of the fact of the existence of God, but not much results from this. On the second level there is the moment of entrusting. When God is trusted, there is the confession of His personal divine nature and the acknowledgment of His veracity, and so there is also the recognition of the truthfulness of the revealed divine Word and of Church teaching based upon it. These two levels of faith do not yet express its fullness, through which there is a total openness toward the justifying supernatural life. Only at the third level does faith cross an essential threshold that ensures its liveliness and spiritual fecundity.

At the third stage faith is formed by supernatural love, and so it enables the expressing of *credo in Deum*: I believe *toward* God. The Latin *in*, which is followed here by the accusative and not the ablative case, denotes *movement* and not merely a location. The translation "I believe *in* God" does not capture the fullness of meaning because there is something more here. *Credo in Deum* could be translated as "I believe toward God," meaning that I set out in His direction. I take hold of myself and tend toward God and, as a result, this focus on Him has an impact on everything I do. At this level faith is formed by charity, and so one tends toward God because He is loved, because there is a friendly relationship with Him and everything is done for Him and in view of Him.

This differentiation of the stages of faith points to an essential threshold between the first two levels and the faith that is formed by charity, which is decisive for the spiritual life. Growth in faith basically means the transfer from unformed faith, in which one only declares the existence of God and recognizes Him as truthful, to a living faith animated by charity, which unites with Him in friendship, and, being a virtue, is creatively transposed on relationships with people, the friends of God. Such a faith tied with charity has an impact on one's entire life.

Christians frequently, even for many years, live only at the first stage. They believe in the existence of God and do not dare to deny His being. They express respect for the Holy Scriptures and the Church. They accept, at least verbally, everything that the Church teaches and do not quarrel with Her about this. But, at the same time, they are not really interested in the divine Word. They do not try to get to know the core of the revealed truths. In fact, they do not care about them at all. They do not attempt to live according to them, even though they do not reject them. What is lacking is the plenitude of faith, the practical living according to the grace of faith. This frequently is due to sin. The Church deems grave sins to be mortal precisely because they kill sanctifying grace in the soul. Those who persist in mortal sin retain the grace of faith, if they have not sinned directly against it, but they lack sanctifying grace, which enables enduring friendship with God. And so their faith is not alive and vibrant.

Sanctifying grace ignites charity in the soul, and so it maintains a dynamic friendship with God. One who believes *toward* God is concerned not only about his eventual arrival in Heaven, but also about the here and now, that there be a friendly relationship with Him. Companionship with God stimulates the will as it urges the intellect to receive Him and to relate to Him in a welcoming way, for His pleasure. It opens up the supernatural fecundity of grace in the soul precisely at the moment when that friendly bond with God is expressed. Grace is then immediately fruitful, both within the believer, and to a certain extent also in bystanders, who, often unawares, are led toward God by the one animated by divine force. A consciously nurtured companionship with God becomes a basic rule of life that has an impact on the entire intellectual and moral life. The believer who lives out an enduring encounter with God not only behaves well, avoiding evil, but also wonders how he can contribute to making something of divine charity visibly present here and now, for the pleasure of God Himself. That is why faith on the third level, animated by the love of God, is a virtuous faith, embracing the entire personality that ardently strives toward God and is open to the dynamism of His grace.

Since faith is a gift of grace, what do we make of those who have not developed it and who remain stuck on the level of belief in the existence of God, recognizing His veracity, but not daring to tend toward Him consciously, with all the consequences that this entails? They believe that God is out there, but they do not know how to love Him truly, or they do not want to do so. Perhaps they are entangled in some emotional or sinful life situation, which prevents them from completely handing themselves over to God and striving toward Him according to His rules. Are such people beyond the grace of God? No! There is grace in them, and so they *do* belong to the Church. They are not to be excluded just because they do not live according to the fullness of faith and do not receive the sacraments.

The Church is for sinners and not just for perfect saints. Thus, those who are not in the state of grace should not be viewed as non-Christians. Divine grace works also at the first two levels of faith. Without it faith would be impossible. Even when faith is not yet formed by supernatural love, true grace is still working in the soul leading it to the highest Good, to which all wills tend. We naturally desire happiness and the attainment of the ultimate end. The desire for Heaven for ourselves is appropriate and good. It sparks the will and, in so doing, awakens the reason to recognize and to believe the highest Good, which is God. As we desire Heaven for ourselves, we believe in the existence of God and commend ourselves to Him. Such a faith is true, and it keeps Christians within the Church, even though they have not yet attained the fullness of sanctity.

In the movement of the will, two moments can be distinguished, both of which are right and proper, even though they are distinct. In the first, there is the desire of the good for oneself. There is nothing dishonest in the fact that we want the good, in particular the highest Good, for ourselves. The desire for Heaven is not a sign of egoism because heavenly happiness is not limited in quantity. As we desire supreme Beatitude coming from God, we do not take it away from anybody. In the second drive of the will there is the extra moment of willing the good of others. In friendship we want the highest true good not only for ourselves, but also for the person we love. When in a relationship the possessing of the other for oneself dominates, with no concern for that person's true good, this is not real friendship but manipulation.

In practical life, of course, these internal drives of the will frequently overlap and cannot be distinguished with precision, as can be done in theoretical reflection. Divine grace works within the will and manifests itself differently, depending on whether one desires the ultimate good for oneself, which mobilizes one toward believing in the existence of God, and trusting in Him, or whether one desires a friendly intercourse with Him for His pleasure, which leads one to believing *toward* Him, for His love. As we differentiate these two movements of the will, we can discern varied workings of grace in the psyche, and so essential stages of faith. These stages depend on whether faith is truly animated by supernatural charity, or whether this has not yet come about.

Using the technical language of speculative theology, Aquinas declared that in acts of charity God is not only the *final end*, but also the *formal reason* of action.[59] This means that good acts are not only to be measured by technical proficiency or even by a natural moral virtue, such as honesty or justice. What is at issue here is that everything is to be done *for God*, in view of Him. Focusing upon God, precisely within the plenitude of faith, involves an actual awareness and recollection of Him, while doing things for Him, out of love. The grasping of this distinction is clear in the love of enemies. It is easier to consciously remember God when, in the gesture of love, there are no other purely human motives. Human reasons and reactions may even be quite contrary, and yet, despite everything, in view of God, the gestures of love are made. It is important, however, that even simple and easy actions be done for the love of God.

In unformed faith the reason accepts the truth about God offered by Him. In the theological virtue of hope the will is attracted to happiness that is expected from God. But in charity, one adheres to God *for Himself*,[60] and then one loves others in view of God. This focus on God impacts faith and transforms it from within, and, as a result, this now-formed faith moves *toward* God. Such supreme, living faith assures immediate openness to the power and grace of God. The vitality of the Church depends above all on the quality of such a living faith.

These speculative theological reflections may seem to be somewhat dry, technical, and excessively theoretical. Locating oneself amidst these distinctions can at times be difficult. But what is essential is not that we know precisely where we or others are on the map leading to sanctity, though the Church does claim that we may assess whether we ourselves are in the state of sanctifying

[59] *Quaestiones disputatae*, *De virtutibus* q. 2, art. 5, ad. 2.

[60] *Summa Theologiae* IIa-IIae, q. 23, art. 6.

grace or not. The Church also knows that there are improper human situations that are a barrier against the plenitude of grace, and so they make the reception of the Eucharist impossible. This, of course, is not a denial of the dignity of such individuals, nor does it throw into doubt the genuine goodness of which they may still be capable. It is also not a rejection of the authenticity of the grace of faith, which may still remain and deepen in those who, on the one hand, believe in the existence of God, earnestly trust Him, and elicit true, generous acts of love and, on the other hand, have broken the marital bond and formed a supposed marriage with somebody else. That is why the Church advises those who have found themselves in such a situation to persist in prayer, adore the Blessed Sacrament, read the Holy Scriptures in faith, and commend themselves to God. In this way, their faith is maintained and may deepen.

In the practical living out of faith by individuals there are multiple conditionings, inhibitions, conscious and unconscious resistances, personal life histories, and obligations deriving from past actions, but this does not mean that theological distinctions, which precisely and speculatively articulate faith and its dynamics, are senseless or unimportant. Terms that are traditionally used in the Church allow us to describe the horizon of the spiritual life and its basic framework, making the struggle toward this perspective possible. The distinction between unformed faith and faith formed by supernatural love has great value, primarily because it makes one aware of the need to be concerned for the quality of faith and its development. This is important so that faith can move beyond the level of declarations and truly influence life, ensuring access to divine grace.

When one remembers that faith enables a contact with God, opening the soul to grace, the divine mystery and power of grace may be introduced into one's entire life, including into its volitional and emotional dimensions—that is, into the spheres of decision-making and coping with one's moods and emotions. By no means is this obvious. Perseverance in a living faith is not automatic, even though it is quite simple and does not require heroic psychic or moral powers. To be trustful and disposed toward God, like a child who counts on receiving gifts, is not something that is notably difficult. But for many adults this specifically is problematic, because they would like to establish their relationship with God in their own way, according to their own convictions.

In the spiritual life, above all, the habit of persisting in union with God, of remembering Him and doing everything for His pleasure has to be developed. When some action is undertaken, either at the initial stage of intention, or in the deliberation about its appropriateness, or in the decision itself, or in the final execution, or else in the struggling against difficulties or laziness, divine light and assistance may be repeatedly invited in faith. In this it is important that one's own projects not be stubbornly forced upon God, but that the divine perception and power be brought into them by faith. This means that personal ideals should not be treated as final or absolutely necessary, but instead there should be an acceptance of God's ways that may differ from one's own plans and designs. The purification of faith should lead to a gradual liberation from attempts to force one's own projects and ideologies upon God. But fear of the temptation of dictating to God one's own view should not slow down the calling of His aid. It is better to turn toward God with a strong will, even when it is bent on something that He does not grant, rather than to ignore Him completely.

The mind may be focused on the external act only, or also on the internal act that is the intention. Both of these movements may be tied with God through a living faith. The important thing is to do everything for God and in Christ, "through Him, with Him and in Him." We generally accept that the most important matters of life are done, not as a result of cold rational calculation, but in trust. Falling in love, contracting a marriage, taking up a vocation, continuing in faithful love even when it turns out to be difficult, the serene withstanding of suffering or illness—all these issues are generally lived out in faith, in an inner acceptance of the unknown and of the mystery that is taking place in life. It is important however that this will be more than just a natural reflex of optimism. The intentional exercise of the divinely received virtue of faith—that is, a conscious focusing on God accompanied by the belief that faith is supernatural—may take place not only in dramatic moments when other reasons and hopes crash, but also in everyday moments. And it is precisely then, as faith is truly expressed in the soul, that grace is set in motion. Being united with God does not necessarily mean that we guarantee to God that everything done will be perfect, unstained by sin. We cannot promise this to God, or even to ourselves. But God does not demand absolute perfection from us. He desires only that we live out our lives with Him, relating to Him, inviting His grace.

Often in moments of weakness, in times of spiritual poverty, we remember and call upon God. We need not be ashamed before ourselves or others that we are feeble and limited. Instead we can use this to deepen our trust in God, so that everything is done in union with Him. "I shall be very happy to make my weaknesses my special boast so that the power of Christ may stay over me" (2 Cor. 12:9). Such a calling upon grace does not mean reckless, irrational action that throws the charge entirely upon God. It requires also human responsibility, the full engagement of one's capacities and talents; one should be childlike and confident toward God, but in the face of challenges one needs to be mature, like an adult. By calling on God and relying on His grace, it is possible to engage in courageous and sometimes risky action, which one might likely avoid if one were to count only on personal forces. When divine grace is the foundation, truly believed as being real, it is possible to hold on to values even when others question them. Then, impossible steps, humanly speaking, become imaginable. The consecrated life is a visible sign for all in the Church that life may be grounded upon God, not only in an instance of youthful fervor, but totally—engaging the whole being, will, affectivity, the desire for independence, riches, and family—and this may be until death. Happy consecrated persons who have handed themselves over to God are a visible sign of the existence of grace.

That God grants the virtue of faith, together with grace, as a result of which all actions can be undertaken in union with God, raises a further question about the faith of baptized infants or of individuals suffering from mental disorders. Since babies do not yet have the developed faculties of the mind and will, are they gifted with the grace of faith? And if so, how can we understand this?

This question has frequently bothered theologians. Aquinas answered it by explaining that a *virtue* differs from an *act*.

An unconscious or sleeping adult does not perform acts of faith and charity centered upon God and yet does not lose the virtue of faith that enables contact with Him. When infants are baptized, they are immersed in God. They receive the grace of the Holy Spirit and infused virtues. The fact that these virtues are still undeveloped, due to the deficiency of the natural spiritual faculties, does not mean that they are nonexistent and that these infants have no grace of faith. When these children grow, the supernatural life will manifest itself. If their faith is nourished and focused, it may become the axis of their lives.

The Church, at the Council of Vienne, declared that this explanation given by Aquinas is most probable.[61] Thus, it is good

[61] *Summa Theologiae* IIIa, q. 69, art. 6. Denzinger and Schönmetzer, *Enchiridion Symbolorum* 904.

to remember that the entire Christian life is an unfolding of the graces of Baptism. At this first sacrament one receives sufficient supernatural resources that can lead to the heights of sanctity, if only one lives in accord with these divine means.

The supernatural life that expresses itself through activated theological virtues is rooted in the natural human faculties. That is why, when the reason and will of the infant are still underdeveloped, the life of faith seems to be dormant. But even at a very early, preschool stage, a little child is capable of some reasoning, of perceiving a moral order and the world of values, of knowing obligations and the experience of respecting them or rebelling against them. A child lives out faith, the offering of oneself to God and relating with Him, even though He is inexpressible, mysterious. Children who observe the prayer of parents are introduced into the world of faith, because they notice that they are not in the center of attention, which is focused elsewhere. This is not only a psychic process of imitating adults or being obedient to their educative influence. The real faith of praying parents establishes a contact with God and opens the channel to divine grace that then passes on to the surroundings. And so the child who has faith in the soul from Baptism is drawn into the atmosphere of grace present in the liturgy and in the prayers of adults and, thus, in some moments, the child can perform acts of faith. In fact, a trustful faith that reaches out toward that which is incomprehensible, but in its mystery is attractive, is easier for a child than for an adult. It is only in later life that psychic resistances against faith appear, and these may derive from a proud conviction about one's self-sufficiency, from the autonomy of the reason, from adherence to sin, or from incorrect views about the relationship to God and accompanying reflexes.

A neurotic individual who is frightened of self, of the emotions, and of God, and who is concentrated primarily with sin, real or imagined, erects a fearful, psychic barrier between the self and God. Such a person lacks a childlike trust in the heart of the heavenly Father. A similar, also neurotic, barrier arises whenever one relies solely on one's own forces, and the passions are experienced as a sphere that has to be completely and immediately subjected to the constraint of moral obligation by the force of emotional energy. Such inhibitions are partly intellectual because they derive from a deformed vision of God, in which there is no place for divine paternity and His warm love. But most often they are emotional, resulting from an acquired distrust of feelings and natural bodily and psychic desires. Like a wedge, this distrust blocks the harmonious cooperation of the passions with reason, will, and grace and impedes union with God. Faith and the other theological virtues should have a prime place in the psyche, but when their primacy is shelved by psychic inhibitions that stop grace from acceding to the intellectual, volitional, and emotional life, then faith remains only on the level of declarations and the deeper psyche, with its morality, continues without the support of grace. Attempts to force order upon oneself without calling upon grace by faith are, of course, futile. The building of moral propriety through natural forces ensures only temporary success and generates constant psychic tension.

Can faith that draws grace, then, bring spiritual and moral healing while such internal resistance continues? The issue boils down to this question: Should moral and psychic disorder be confronted first so that psychic space is opened up for faith and the spiritual life, or should the spiritual life be embarked upon first, leading to a trustful and loving encounter with God through faith and grace, so that psychic and moral healing could then come about? But how can one open up to the plenitude of faith, precisely when there is a barrier in the psyche against it? Many individuals entangled in some addiction struggle with this question. Experience proves that the multiplication of prayers does not in itself liberate one from addictions, and psychiatric treatment without a spiritual life generally focuses on self and does not necessarily bring liberation.

The problem is not to be resolved from an either-or perspective. Undoubtedly, correcting erroneous thinking about morals, specifically one that excessively stresses moral obligation with an insufficient emphasis on the life of grace, is an enormous help. However, this should not be mistaken for a rejection of all moral teaching whatsoever. This issue is not played out uniquely on the level of knowledge, even theological knowledge. What is decisive is the authentic living by grace. When faith is animated by charity focused upon God, it trustfully counts upon divine aid. It recognizes the working of the grace of the Holy Spirit and turns toward God with the attitude of a child who relates to the Father without paralyzing fear (see Rom. 8:14–17). Where there is lively faith, there is a transfer of psychic and moral difficulties from one's own shoulders to the shoulders of Christ the Savior. Thus, the practice of contemplative prayer liberates from anxiety and allows one to rest in God. Certainly, the intellectual understanding of mechanisms of repression is helpful. This may be an emotional repression that blocks the power of an undesired passion by the force of another repressing passion. It may be an intellectual-ideological repression that excludes the mystery of faith from the life of the intellect. And, finally, there may be a spiritual repression that denies grace access to all dimensions of life.

The life of faith is a constant calling upon divine grace, and so there is no need to panic after mistakes. They can be treated with humor. Individuals who are concentrated on personal errors are very serious about themselves and cannot laugh at their blunders. Faith is a joyful and trustful attachment to God, and so it allows for a playful, friendly relationship for His pleasure. When St. Teresa of Avila was going through difficulties in the establishment of convents, she humorously pointed out to God that if that is the way He treats His friends, it is not surprising that He has so few of them! Maturity in faith does not guarantee complete and permanent psychic and moral perfection. And so some rough edges may appear that should not provoke panic. There are weaknesses that we carry throughout all our lives. It is important, however, that we bear them in union with God. Maybe He has left them in us so as to prevent our falling into proud self-sufficiency and to inspire continual childlike returning to God in which His paternal support is counted on. Eventually, basing one's life on God, expecting His grace in all dimensions of life, brings psychic equilibrium with it.

Since the supernatural life is a real life, it may happen that it dies out. When faith is formed by charity, it is actively and consciously focused upon God. This may continue even in a habitual state. When one is not thinking about God in a given moment, not actively directing oneself to Him, the virtue of faith persists. Then, when an occasion appears, active faith toward Him may again be expressed out of love. This capacity for a relationship with God is destroyed by grave sin, which precisely for this reason is termed "mortal." Its essence consists in the fact that it kills the life of grace in the soul. When acts contrary to the law of God are committed consciously and willingly, this entails, even though maybe only momentarily, a rejection of God, because something else is chosen as the most important end. This refusal of God kills the life of faith. Such a person then needs not healing, but *resurrection*.

The return to sanctifying grace cannot come about through natural action, because human nature cannot elevate itself to the level of the supernatural. Only an injection of grace enables a return to God. Without doubt, the sacrament of Penance brings the supernatural life back to the soul, but this may happen before the reception of the sacrament. When God in His goodness grants an interior grace—which results in a renewed focus toward God out of love for Him, alone, and not only out of a desire for salvation—such a turning to God in pure love with perfect contrition, consciously expressed, that includes the resolution to have recourse to the sacrament when possible, restores the life of grace. There is, however, a difference between perfect contrition and the reception of the sacrament of Penance. Contrition is very subjective and does not grant the certitude that the return to God has been true, really out of love of Him. Sacramental absolution received from the hands of a priest grants internal certitude that the return to the orbit of grace has taken place.

Mortal sins kill the life of grace, but they do not necessarily kill faith. An unformed faith, one that does not focus upon God out of love, but believes that He exists and is truthful, remains after mortal sin. It is thanks to this faith that the supernatural life may be reborn. But when a sin goes directly against faith, then faith is excluded from the soul. Sins that reject God—the sins of atheism, blasphemy, or heresy (in which there is a picking and choosing what truths of the faith to accept, abolishing the motive of faith that is the authority of the self-revealing God)—destroy faith. Without a special gift of grace such a sinner will not raise himself back to a living faith.

The nourishments of faith

We read in the Gospels about three foods for eternal life. Jesus said about Himself: "I am the living bread which has come down from heaven. Anyone who eats this bread will live forever" (John 6:51) and "My food is to do the will of the one who sent me and to complete his work" (John 4:34). And He answered the tempter saying: "Man does not live on bread alone but on every word that comes from the mouth of God" (Matt. 4:4).

Not only the Eucharist, but all the sacraments are material signs through which grace is truly given. Thanks to them faith is nourished and strengthened in the soul. They are not just symbols reminding us about a permanent divine gift: God truly gives Himself when the sacraments are received. Aquinas decidedly rejected the interpretation that stresses only the moral and not the physical causality of the sacraments.[62] Of course, what is meant here is not the modern empirical science of physics, but the objective divine gift that is always granted whenever the sacraments are administered.

When the emphases are shifted and the factual and objective working of God in the sacraments is forgotten, then prime attention is focused on the catechetical dimension that accompanies sacramental celebrations or, even worse, on their social or even artistic aspect. It is true that during Mass the Word of God is read and then explained by the priest. It is true that the faithful gather for celebrations and the liturgical setting has its beauty. The First Holy Communion of a child or a wedding is an occasion to meet with family and friends. But this is not most important. What is most important is the gift of God Himself.

The center of the Eucharistic liturgy is neither the priest nor the gathered community, but Christ Himself, who gives Himself out of love. His gift of self, handed over to the heavenly Father and to us, identical to the sacrifice rendered once and for all on the Cross, is the source of grace. The sinner who is conscious that evil needs to be punished and repaired in the name of justice may be freed from sin whenever he holds on to the sacrifice of the Cross that is made available to him. That is why the sacrifice of the Cross is constantly offered on the altars of the Church: so that we would

[62] *Summa Theologiae* IIIa, q. 62, art. 1.

not forget about this total oblation of Christ, and so that we will profit from it.

Where the primacy of Christ is forgotten and the main emphasis falls not on His sacrifice, in which the priest is to be concealed, but either on the priest who presides over the liturgy or on the community that gathers and celebrates itself, churches quickly become empty. If the priest is in the center, immediately the question is raised: What is the value of a liturgy when it turns out that he is not particularly interesting, not very intelligent and witty, and even a sinner? And if the community that celebrates itself is in the center, then what meaning does it have for young people, who can say that the elderly people in the church do not interest them and they find a better communitarian spirit in a club, coffee shop, or pub?

In the sacraments God objectively gives Himself and invisible, but real, divine grace is infused into the soul. The sacramental liturgy is captivating only when it is clear that above all it is an encounter with God.

Whenever one receives a sacrament, there is always an objective change in the soul. The supernatural life initiated and set into motion by active faith is nourished and enlivened by the sacraments. Some sacraments introduce a permanent change in the receiver irrespective of the quality of faith at the moment the sacrament is received, and irrespective of the faith of the one who administers it. In Baptism, Confirmation, Matrimony, and Holy Orders a new objective quality appears in the receiver which lasts until death. God enters into a covenant with the individual in an irrevocable and specific way, and this is confirmed by the validly received sacrament. Human infidelity, weakness, and sinfulness do not call into question God's gift and the promise of His future graces that are available whenever the individual reaches out and engages in a relationship with Him through faith and charity. The objectivity of the sacraments, therefore, grants a certitude that can be the grounding of life. Spouses joined by the sacrament of Matrimony know that their way to Heaven is through one another and that they have no other way. While the question of the validity of the sacraments is essential at the moment of their reception, afterward, in life, it is more important to be aware of their fecundity and to profit from them by vivifying them in faith and prayer.

When exercised faith calls to mind the received sacrament, graces flowing from it are applied to the current situation in life and to its challenges. It is impossible to persevere in a vocation and in the journey to sanctity without the power of the sacraments, called forth by faith. The graces of Baptism, Matrimony, and Holy Orders need to be *lived out*. They are enlivened by prayer and the reception in faith of the sacraments of Penance and the Eucharist.

The quality of faith does not impact the validity of the sacraments—and, anyway, how could that quality be measured? But it does have an influence on their fruitfulness. On the one hand, the reception of the sacraments with faith extends their fecundity and, on the other hand, the sacraments themselves are a food for faith that deepens it. Sacraments nourish faith in the soul, facilitate performing its acts, and encourage a reliance on the mystery of the living God. The believer who receives the sacraments may stand fast on the solid foundation that is the mystery of faith that sets grace in motion. Sometimes this is difficult, in particular when the adversities of life tempt one to try to escape from God and His guidance. But perseverance in faith, the grounding of oneself on its foundation, knowing that it is elusive yet true, allows one to grow in the supernatural life that ultimately is the eternal life.

Just as Christ is the incarnate Word of God sent to us, so the Holy Scriptures contain that divine Word. That Word is anterior to the Scriptures and is not exhausted in them: It existed before all the Scriptures were written. God continues to send His Word to human hearts, and it becomes sustenance for faith. When the Scriptures are read, they have to be read as the Word of God—that is, in faith centered upon Christ. The Paschal Mystery of Jesus, His total gift of self, and the light of the Holy Spirit focus the reading of the Scriptures and illuminate their deepest meaning. Of course, there is room for exegetical studies that specify the proper literary form of a given book of the Bible (or part of it), perceive their historical context, and explain the correct meaning of words. All this scientific apparatus, conscientiously applied to the text of the Scriptures, is precious—but it is only ancillary. The believer who opens the Holy Scriptures on the lap is looking for something more than just historical information or a story. The person of faith is looking for, or rather listening to, what God is saying. Such a reading of the Scriptures in faith allows one to hear the divine word addressed to oneself, and so it nourishes faith and accustoms one to the reception of the life-giving mystery.

All other teaching offered in the Church, whether from popes, councils, preachers, or theologians—and also from teachers and parents—is to be received in the same spirit. God uses human words to transmit His Word. It is therefore important that preachers and theologians remember that above all they are teachers of faith.

St. Thomas Aquinas, quoting St. Augustine in the opening lines of his greatest theological work, declared that sacred teaching has four functions: It is to generate, to nourish, to strengthen, and to defend life-giving faith.[63] Faith, of course, is not born directly from theology. It is a gift of God, but theology, like a mother, is to transmit the life of faith. Then, again, like a mother, it is to nourish faith, supplying subject matter that will form mental structures

[63] *Summa Theologiae* Ia, q. 1, art. 2, sc.

within the received divine mystery and ignite the will and heart to a life that is in accord with it. Theology is then to strengthen faith just as food makes one strong. When faith seems to be torn apart, when foreign views are on the verge of submerging it, the intellectual certitude that derives from the knowledge of the truths of faith allows one to find support in these truths. And, finally, theological teaching serves to defend faith against contrary winds that may extinguish it.

Theological thought has to be also attentive to questions raised by the world and surrounding culture. It has to engage with them, discerning typical resistances against faith, noting their sources, and untangling misunderstandings and mental habits that deform or obscure faith. This effort is difficult, but it has to be done in every time and culture. Its aim, however, is not to adapt faith to currently fashionable views so as to agree with them or to make faith accessible to them. Theology is to transmit not the fancies of the theologian. It has to be rooted in God Himself, who has shared His Word with us.

The questions that theology deals with have to be real, arising from an actual context and the difficult struggles of contemporary people. But the answers should not be arbitrary. They have to be sought within the great tradition of the Church. A renewal of theological thinking always consists in the transfer from a superficial reaction to a problem to a deeper understanding of it in the light of the great tradition that corrects and explains it. It is not a question of having some museum-type knowledge of ancient questions and ancient answers, but of having a deeper and closer adherence to the living God. That is why it is not possible to engage in theological thinking without a simultaneous encounter with God, maintained through a living faith. A professional competence in Church teaching, both present and past, with no authentic spiritual life, is possible, but the lack of a vivid faith makes it discomforting. Teaching in the Church has to grow out of faith, out of the divine Word received in faith, so that it can nourish it. That is why theologians and preachers have to be humble, knowing that they are only secondary causes and the prime cause is always God, Who makes use of human effort. Only then, through the effort of the preacher of faith are the faithful disposed to receive the grace of the Holy Spirit and to learn how to apply it in life.

The faithful are often confused by the flood of materials, information, views, and investigations that frequently are inconsistent and changeable. When they turn to some biblical commentaries or complex and difficult theological works that do not immediately nourish faith, even more so, they do not know what to judge and to think. There is then the temptation to hold on to something light or some supposedly miraculous event, or to base oneself on the opinion of someone close, whom one then endows with decisive authority. But that close friend may sometimes be a disappointment. It is good to listen to the voice of pastors, but when what they have to say seems futile, or not particularly interesting, one need not panic or complain. An educated person has to be personally and seriously concerned about faith and should not wait until somebody serves proper food for it. Faith has to be childlike toward God, but it also has to be the faith of an adult. This means that one has to care for one's faith, searching out good nourishment for it. One should not grumble against pastors, because they have to speak to people who are very diverse and have differing levels of education and spiritual life, and so what they say does not always touch the present needs of the heart or answer burning questions. Each of us has to ensure that personal faith is formed and deepened by the true doctrine of the Church, which is greater and more profound than the teaching of an assistant pastor in the local parish.

It is good, therefore, to hold on to a great master. We rarely find one among the living. So we have to turn to the great witnesses of faith of the past who pondered the divine mysteries. This is not easy, because they lived in varying epochs and used terms and images that were contemporary to them, which spoke to the people of their times, and which are not necessarily clear today. But it is important that all who are concerned about the faith, in particular a priest or religious, male or female, should hold on to a great master, choosing such a teacher of faith who is meaningful and is confirmed by the authority of the Church. This may be St. Augustine, St. Thomas Aquinas, St. John of the Cross, St. Thérèse of Lisieux, or somebody closer to our times, such as St. John Paul II or Benedict XVI.

One could, for instance, study carefully all the encyclicals and apostolic exhortations of St. John Paul II, as well as their commentaries, asking questions about the difficulties, challenges, and theological debates in the Church at that time, and about the pope's response to them. Such a study undertaken in one's own rhythm, for oneself, without thinking about academic degrees, will form mental structures and reflexes of the will and heart, generating a prime place for faith.

Some writers can be read for some time, even for several years, and then comes the time when there is the need to look for something different and deeper. Others, like the great masters, may be studied throughout a lifetime. If a young priest takes hold of St. Augustine and, in the space of two decades, reads all his major writings and studies secondary works that explain his doctrine and, then, consequently, if all his sermons, retreats, catechesis, and articles are based on the teaching of the bishop of Hippo, the young priest will not be confused. Such a priest will deal not only with current themes raised by the vociferous media. He will respond not only to those questions, usually simple ones, that people raise. He himself will address his own questions to the great tradition of the Church. Immersed in it and in its light, he will understand better how to lead himself and how to direct others better. If such a study is accompanied by true prayer, the priest will not go astray, and he will have food not only for his own faith, but also for the faith of those who have been committed to him.

Jesus' confession that the fulfillment of the will of the Father is nourishment for Him is a lesson for us. It is true that throughout His earthly life Jesus enjoyed the Beatific Vision, and so we cannot speak about His *faith*—but His execution of the works of the Father shows how our faith can be strengthened. Faith is made robust not only by confessing it, but also by following it practically in life. As faith opens toward God, it lights a little flame on the path of life. It is not strong and dazzlingly bright but, rather, is like the cloud that led the chosen people across the waters of the Red Sea and through the desert. The awareness of the fact that the waters could crash was probably terrifying, but in spite of this, the Israelites continued to march on toward the Promised Land. This journey was not straightforward, as the actual distance between the places might suggest: One can hike from Egypt to Palestine in a week. Instead, it was a circuitous wandering across the desert for forty years—but always following God. During this time something happened to the Israelites: They recognized that they were the people of God. They became aware of their covenant with God and received the Law from Him.

Our life's journey is just such a trip, in which we recognize the divine light in faith and then follow it. What is our true vocation? And which moment in our life will turn out to be the most important? We will probably find out the answers to these questions at the moment of death. God leads us on the way of faith, in which there are lucid moments but, most of the time, there is the obscurity of the mystery of faith. God does not expect idleness; He wants us to walk by faith, even though most of the time we do not have clarity as to the way. We go through life like a bird flying in the sky, and so we ourselves have to set the route. Sometimes it is good to stop for a moment and check whether we are going in the right direction. A retreat or break spent in different surroundings with time for rest and prayer may be helpful but, in sum, we go through life following a way that is dark and hazy.

There are times when God draws us with great force, and the discernment of our basic vocation is clear. The contracting of a marriage, the vowing of a religious profession, or the reception of Holy Orders grants certitude as to our direction. But then the needs of the day and further stages of life are not so obvious. Decisions of superiors, family challenges, and steps that had already been made give structure to life. But how is life to be lived out, and which issues are most important? This has to be perceived in faith. God is not holding in His hand a disc on which our life has been recorded in advance. God awaits our courageous and independent steps, undertaken in faith, counting upon His support, in union with Him. One thing is sure: Our way of life is totally different from what we could have ever imagined or planned. God is leading us and expecting that we will be attentive and faithful to His voice. But He is constantly surprising us. In this bold advance in faith, but without the stubborn imposition of our own ideas upon God, there is the fulfillment of the will of God. At the same time, this is an expression of practical faith and, in turn, nourishment for it. As we hold on to God, we grow in Him and our faith is strengthened.

Theology distinguishes one more extra support that nourishes faith, and they come as if from without, even though they are, in fact, directly given by God. These are the gifts of the Holy Spirit. They are permanent dispositions, points of contact between the individual and the Third Person of the Trinity. At the beginning there is always faith, which enables the encounter with God and sets the supernatural life in motion. Once faith is alive, animated by the love of God (i.e., the relationship with Him is authentic), then these internal capacities which recognize divine promptings are turned on. Through the gifts of the Holy Spirit the believer perceives additional divine lights and encouragements. They are like explanations and counsels sent personally by God that stimulate specific actions.

The gifts of the Holy Spirit solicit a response to be expressed in new gestures of love, and in active and creative generosity. Since they are incentives, they have to be recognized in some way. If they were unidentifiable, they would not spur us on to action. However, they are not lucid like the light of natural reason. The gifts of the Holy Spirit are always interpreted in faith, and so they participate in its obscurity and in the elusiveness of the spiritual life. We have to remember that God seems to us as timid, and so He grants few such hints, in particular when the willingness to answer them is lacking. God does not want to place us in the awkward situation in which the divine invitation meets with our refusal. So only when His request meets a generous response does He urge us further on. In time the call of grace becomes more demanding, leading to a deeper encounter with God and to a more authentic charity.

Where is God leading each individual? This is a mystery. Everything takes place within faith, which is and remains obscure, and so it is never known in advance through what stages, struggles, difficulties, and turnings of our personal vocation we will have to pass. God writes straight on the crooked ways of men, and whoever is attentive to divine appeals and responds to them generously is led ever more toward eternity. The road with God in which the Holy Spirit's signals are received is always the way of faith. Only in Heaven will the light of glory allow for a lucid relationship with God.

As he tried to specify the particular working of the Holy Spirit that supports faith, Aquinas pointed to two of His gifts: that of understanding and knowledge. The clarification of the Holy Spirit's work on this level necessarily cannot be exact. The more the movements of grace are studied, the more there is a reaching out beyond that which can be known sensitively and mentally. That is why the description of this mystery is hazy. Faith as it is formed by charity becomes open to a further action of the gifts of the Holy Spirit.

The gift of understanding, termed *intellectus* in Latin, corresponds in part to the intellect, and so to that natural function of the mind, in which there is a direct grasping of the known truth. Just as the intellect reads into the known reality, in this gift of the Holy Spirit there is an *intus legere* (reading inwardly), allowing one to grasp the mysterious reality and penetrate it. This is closer to the functioning of the *intellect* than of the *reason*, because natural reason, as distinct from the intellect, arrives at perception through a process in which it aligns everything exactly and logically. This gives reason the upper hand over knowledge. Meanwhile this gift of the Holy Spirit calms the reason so that it will not manipulate and interfere with God's action and, instead, will agree to God's leading it further on and deeper than what it, on its own, can grasp. Some people do not need additional reasons and arguments for the deepening of their faith. On the contrary, they have to have the courage to stop basing themselves uniquely upon reasons and arguments and, instead, to open up their mind so that it will face directly a reality that transcends it (Ps. 24:7).

This gift of the Holy Spirit penetrates the mystery of faith, drawing the mind way beyond those limits in which it feels safe trusting in its own forces. Thanks to the work of the Holy Spirit in the soul, the believer can immediately grasp the meaning of a mysterious truth and distinguish it from falsehood. An appreciation of the significance of the Resurrection of Christ or of the role of the

Eucharist is not just the result of a reasoned learning of catechetical truths. He who truly believes goes deeper into God out of love of Him and grasps the point of the truth of faith directly, even if such an individual does not possess theological knowledge or is not well versed in the writings of the mystics. The Holy Spirit, present in the soul of the believer, attunes the soul directly toward the truth.

The gift of knowledge, termed *scientia,* supports faith from without, allowing it to pass judgments about the truths of faith or about some pending task. As one reads into a truth, one faces that truth directly. But when cognitive judgments are made, the process of thinking ends, and since the matter is known, one arrives at a conclusion. The gift of knowledge, deriving from the Holy Spirit, allows for a similar closing of the mental discourse within faith. Then, in the light of faith, one not only knows the truth but also knows what one *needs to do* for the love of God. The task of this gift can be said to consist in training a sense of faith, which can immediately distinguish what is in accord with faith from what is contrary to it, or what undercuts its force. This support of the Holy Spirit grants certitude in faith. Thanks to it, faith becomes strong and resistant against contrary views. Since the gifts of the Holy Spirit offer their impulses only when faith is formed by charity—the love of God and of people in view of God—the certitude deriving from the gift of knowledge differs from an aggressive ideological stubbornness. This certitude is located within charity, and so it is serene and perseverant. In the name of this certitude the believer does not give up charity and so persists in truth, even if other people do not see it or even reject it.

After he had discussed the three theological virtues and their contrary sins, Aquinas mentioned one more gift of the Holy Spirit, that of wisdom, or *sapientia,* which also influences faith. This wisdom, coming directly from the Holy Spirit, acts like the culmination of the harmony introduced into the soul by grace and as a consequence of the primacy of faith, hope, and charity. Divine wisdom allows one to assess everything from the highest vantage point, and it generates delight in this godly perspective. The believer united completely with God is led by His wisdom and participates in it. Faith assents to truths revealed by God, whereas the wisdom that is a gift of the Holy Spirit extends deeper, because it allows for judging everything in a divine way, according to the criterion that is the wisdom of God Himself.[64]

These attempts to describe the workings of the gifts of the Holy Spirit are only approximate. They remind us that since the theological virtues are a divine gift, their functioning in the soul is nourished by a direct divine intervention. Viewed intellectually, there is nothing surprising in the fact that supernatural faith seeks supernatural support. In practical life this expresses itself in the fascinating and surprising adventure of living with God, as we advance full of childlike trust. "Everyone moved by the Spirit of God is a son of God" (Rom. 8:14).

The purifications of faith

Faith must be not only nourished but also purified from that which is foreign to it. As it is infused in the soul, faith enables assent to God as the First Truth. Faith draws with it hope and charity, but for this to happen, and for these truly to be the basic criteria of thinking, acting, and feeling, these virtues have to be freed from distortions. The supernatural life, even though it is subtle and hidden (but strong), is frequently intermingled with personal ideas, ideologies, reflexes, natural hopes and aspirations, and a feeling of self-sufficiency. The theological virtues focus upon God, and so, in their essence, they connect with Him and ensure that He is truly

[64] *Summa Theologiae* IIa-IIae, q. 45, art. 1 ad. 2.

the One who supports us with His power and leads us through life. Faith makes one aware that one can turn to God whenever personal weakness is experienced, but also that it is possible to rely upon Him in everything that one does, and always, even in situations when one does not feel weak. Thus, God should not be cast aside under the conviction that we can manage everything without Him. Of course, many life situations *can be* dealt with without God, but a true fruitfulness of what we do, in the name of the most important values that lead to ultimate happiness, is possible only when faith has called upon the living God. And so He has to be invited into actions, afflictions, and successes. It is through such spiritual life that the Church grows.

Charity enables befriending God, but He has to be the leading figure in this relationship. This does not always come about easily, because sometimes other issues and people become idols that screen God. We have to love people, and in this love there is place for human attachment and concern, but people, even the closest, are not God. They therefore have to be loved in God, desiring for them the supreme true good that is union with God. They have to be loved through God, as His friends who are loved by Him, and it is precisely for this reason that they are to be loved by us. Reference to God defends against a possessive, manipulative treatment of others or a dependence on them such that God becomes unnecessary. By placing God in the center, one can then accept that friends part when relationships are weakened, and in the final transfer to eternity.

Since faith is a divine tool that sets the supernatural life in motion, it is essential that this tool be unmixed with other aspirations. That is why purifications are necessary. We can distinguish two types: the active and the passive.

In active purification the individual becomes aware that in some dimension of life God does not have the primary place. This discovery urges one toward an examination of conscience and taking steps to regain the proper focus. After this inspection, one makes decisions in an attempt to correct or to change something. We do not need great experience to note that, on the whole, such steps are not very successful. Self-imposed religious practices, reading books, and attending a retreat are all conducive toward a renewed relationship with God, but some hidden psychic resistances against Him remain. If conversion is not to be superficial, something deeper has to happen.

Passive purifications are conducted by God Himself. Take, for example, someone who, for many years, is attached to God. This person does not deny faith but recognizes and practices it while fulfilling religious duties. The vocation, which has come from God and is confirmed by received sacraments, is not questioned. But everything is done as if on a superficial level. The relationship with God is maintained by the rules of propriety and a polite agreement not to stand in each other's way. This means that all the spheres of life—of the psyche, dreams, plans, and concrete acts—are played out independently without God and His grace, and so with an internal and frequently unconscious pride. Sometimes the fear of being viewed as silly by friends or renowned intellectuals becomes more important than the integrity of faith. At times ambition leads to an exaggerated concern for good ties with the media or politicians, because this can bring some measurable profit, even for the Church. Thus, there is an attempt to ingratiate oneself with those who are on the crest of popularity in order to attain publicity. Occasionally in the soul there is fear of being caught in some moral weakness, and this lowers the trust of faith. In sum, all these attitudes represent a retreat from the fullness of faith and from the courage of faith that, based on grace, is willing to accept rejection or martyrdom in whatever form they may come. And so, as a result, one strong temptation is sufficient for the entire edifice of devotions to crack.

This is so because years of mediocre religiosity were tolerated and some hidden compromises were made with that which is not God and which obscures Him. All this continues up to some moment . . .

There comes a time when God Himself seems bored with superficial, ostentatious piety, with the lack of authenticity and practical indifference toward Him, and so He intervenes. Thus, a moment of crisis comes that forces change. The wounds of the soul, supposedly closed and healed, suddenly show up, and it is God Who provokes their renewed opening. Such a moment generates anxiety and even consternation, but should not cause panic. It is normal for couples to experience crises in marriage, and difficult moments come in vocations. For years everything was so joyful, simple, and easy, and then suddenly something bursts, and it is terrifying. A crisis is a stage that compels making a serious step forward, toward God. It is no longer possible to drag on in the life of faith, as before. A crisis requires change: Either a decisive step is taken toward God, toward sanctity, or one goes in the opposite direction, where there will be tragedy, the crashing of a vocation, the breaking of a marriage, the dying out of religious life. In a crisis one sees that it is no longer possible to stay put, because this is no option. A continued persistence in superficial religiosity is impossible (see Rev. 3:15–16). It is precisely in such moments that it becomes clear whether faith truly is the foundation of life or whether it was only elegantly declared but, in fact, did not fulfill its function of setting the supernatural life in motion, because it was lost among other issues that were deemed to be more important.

The crisis that God permits is a singular time of grace. God Himself then purifies the faith, and one has to succumb passively to His action. This involves a deepening of faith and the discernment that one has to rely on God alone. The crisis is to be lived out in union with God, believing that His hands are close. This is a time of intensive prayer, until the habit of searching for divine aid is deepened. At the same time, one may experience the proximity of God and the authenticity of His grace. A profound step toward God, in view of Him, is a true turn toward sanctity. Before this stage, the thought of sanctity, of a true reliance upon God, lingered somewhere on the horizon, but with no great urgency or focus. But then the crisis revealed that in the Church there is no other way than that of sanctity; from this one cannot escape. Well, one can escape, and very easily, but this flight ends in tragedy, in the shattering of one's life and sometimes the destruction of other people's lives too.

Spiritual theology distinguishes between two basic thresholds in the passive purification of faith. First there comes the dark night of the senses, and then, sometimes after a long interval, the dark night of the spirit. The dark night of the senses is a time when the difficulty of controlling the emotional sphere is laid bare. It may happen, for example, that during his younger years and time of formation, a priest had no major difficulty in maintaining chastity and controlling his emotions, but five years after his ordination he suddenly falls into some sensual dependency, or is tormented by temptations, or feels the unexpected emergence of ambitions, or experiences sadness and resentment against others and difficulties in his interpersonal relationships. Where does all this come from, since earlier everything seemed to run so smoothly? It is similar in married life. After initially falling in love, after the fascination of engagement and a wonderful wedding, after the joy of living together, and after coming to terms with building a common life, unpredictable difficulties explode: discouragement, the surprise that the other person is so different, the discovery of one's own and the other's egoism, and maybe the temptation of infidelity. Where does all this come from? In addition, external unpredicted, unplanned difficulties may generate tensions: sudden illnesses, financial constraints, economic and social crises, unemployment, or even wars, which all impact personal life, setting it on unexpected tracks. Where is all this leading to? When God allows such difficult moments to happen, the person is faced with the necessity of rooting himself in Him through a deeper and more authentic faith. The purification of faith consists in more than just the untangling of its content from contrary views that divert it from God. This does have to happen, but what is more important is the purity of authentic faith in the soul as it unites to God and becomes absolutely convinced that only He can be totally relied upon, more than anybody or anything else. Such a growing surrender to God alone means holding on to faith, which is, and will be, obscure.

St. Paul went through some difficulty unknown to us, which he called the "thorn in the flesh" (2 Cor. 12:7). Three times he pleaded with God to be liberated from this trial, but he heard that he would not be freed from it. Rather, he was to rely upon the grace that he had already received, which was sufficient. This is so, even though the power of grace is not something that is felt, and sometimes there is the impression that it is escaping through the fingers. This was a divine invitation to persevere in faith and to profit from the humiliation that accompanies weaknesses, because their recognition, tied with faith, leads to a deeper reliance upon God. Finally, St. Paul cried out: "So I shall be very happy to make my weaknesses my special boast so that the power of Christ will stay over me.... For it is when I am weak that I am strong" (2 Cor. 12:9–10). Commenting on this confession of the Apostle, Aquinas noted that God sometimes allows us to fall into some weakness, or even into mortal sin, so that finally we are freed from pride and recognize that we cannot count on our own forces but, instead, have to immerse ourselves in God.[65]

[65] *Super Secundam Epistolam ad Corinthios lectura*, c. 12, l. 3 (472).

There is no rule as to when one passes through the crisis known as the dark night of the senses. It may happen during the youthful stage of puberty, or it may come about during the midlife crisis of a forty-year-old or at the time of menopause—though it is not necessarily tied to physiological changes. Some saints experienced a profound spiritual purification that deeply united them with God way back in their childhood. What is important is persistence in attachment to God through deepened prayer. The aid of a close friend who is knowledgeable in the ways of God, or the support of a spiritual director, may help in navigating this difficult stage. Finally, it needs to be understood that we do not have to be perfect and without stain according to our proud imagination, but we need to unite our poverty with the power and love of God, on whom we can rely through a lively faith.

Generally, after the crisis called the dark night of the senses there is a period of calm. The spiritual experiences have made one aware of the need constantly to return to God. Difficulties in the transmission of faith and values are then recognized as signs of spiritual poverty, from which one may profit, because helplessness tied with trustful faith ensures the fruitfulness of grace in what one does and says. The experience of spiritual poverty is very precious for the pastor because it liberates one from pride and from an angry resentment at people who are far away from God. It allows for a constant calling on divine grace by faith in every encounter, sermon, or celebrated liturgy.

Those who have experienced the passive purification called the dark night of the senses may, after a period of calm, come across a new stage called the dark night of the spirit. Union with God takes place through faith that must become increasingly pure, leading uniquely toward Him. There come moments, even in those who are known to have a strong faith, when their faith seems to crumble, when powerful temptations against it appear, when faith becomes extremely difficult, entrapped by contrary arguments—and yet despite everything, it is heroically maintained, even though external persecutions or scandals in the Church or advancing illnesses lead to the limits of despair. In these trials, it is God Himself who is purifying the faith ever more deeply so that the person will come to rely uniquely and completely upon Him. Those who, in the poverty of this affliction of the dark night of the spirit, in which everything seems to be bursting, remain heroically attached to God, open up streams of grace through the quality of their faith, which bring new life to the Church. The Church is renewed not by great actions, massive events, and costly apostolic plans, but by the quality of faith of those who, in the humility of the spirit, remain attached to God. It is such hidden souls, united with God, who support the Church. Sometimes in a religious community that is having multiple difficulties, the light of faith that brings down grace is carried by one individual who might be old or alone, but who is deeply prayerful.

Passive purifications are directed by God Himself, who allows crises to take place not only in the life of individuals but also in entire local churches. After times of great ecclesial success, with vast building projects and enormous organizational efforts and numerous vocations to the priesthood and religious life—and, even more so, after a time of proud planning of renewal and reform in the Church according to purely human ideas—there comes a moment of crisis. At times, entire countries fall away. Vocations dry up, religious orders and dioceses die out, and people turn away from the Church as they succumb to moral and spiritual nihilism. Bishops and theologians often do not know how to respond. In each country, such a purification of the local Church has its own cultural, social, and political tenor. The reaction should not be one of despair or of a search for culprits. In the spirit of faith, the hand of God has to be discerned in all of this, forcing conversion.

A passive purification, provoked by a crisis, turns out to be salutary. That which is not divine but is a superficial façade crashes. Only those remain who are attached to God and who are really concerned about Him. Their living, purified faith and charity focused upon God ignite the sources of water welling up to eternal life (see John 4:14). It is such supernatural life, deriving from God, that renews the Church.

6

And What About the Unbelievers?

The grace of faith

When in modern centuries people forgot that faith is a gift of God, they concluded logically that it derives from natural human effort, as if it could be forced upon themselves and others. This meant that faith could be generated through conclusive arguments or could come about from mere willing that results from conviction or listening. Thus, in thinking and preaching about faith, its possession was treated as a moral duty, and its lack as the failure to fulfill that duty, which supposedly had to stem directly from the furnished arguments. In such reasoning, the question of unbelievers necessarily appeared. What about those who do not believe, or who believe feebly, or who used to believe and now have stopped believing, or who never had a chance to believe because they died in infancy or in their mother's womb or never heard the voice of someone preaching faith? What will happen with the Chinese who have not yet been evangelized? Since faith is necessary for salvation, does this mean that unbelievers will not be saved? These questions are justified, but to answer them, their presupposition has to be corrected—and then they cease to be so acute.

It is true that through listening (Rom. 10:17) we come to know the content of faith, deduced from the revealed Word of God and transmitted by the Church. But the very capacity of the human spirit to adhere, with the mind and will, to that which one hears—and so to God, the First Truth, and in consequence to trust in Him and to love Him—comes from divine grace. Thus, the reception of this grace often precedes hearing.[66] *First*, the unbeliever is moved by divine grace toward God. *Only then*, and as a result of this, is there a disposition to hear the preached word and to accept it in faith. An infant receives the grace of faith at Baptism, but he hears about the content of faith later on, when he has grown. Faith appears in the soul as a divine gift given according to the generosity and measure of God. Thus, this divine gifting is uneven, dependent on His good pleasure. We notice that the spontaneous impulse of referring to God is easy for some, whereas others arrive at it only after many years. But the development of received faith, which normally enhances the reflex of relating to God, requires the practice of faith that is primarily internal. It thus involves consciously and repeatedly making of acts of faith. When one persists in faith, nourishes it, and grows in the habit of focusing it toward God, faith then grows in the soul. As a consequence, the quality and depth of faith varies greatly among individuals.

Generally, it is acknowledged that faith is necessary for salvation. But salvation is often treated as something on the distant horizon that will come about only after death. Thus, we conclude that for the moment there is no point in thinking about it. The subject might come up when death is approaching. But since general economic prosperity offers self-sufficiency, and progress in medicine has pushed the specter of death further away, thinking about salvation

[66] St. Thomas Aquinas, *Super Epistolam ad Romanos lectura*, c. 10, l. 2 (844).

and life after death does not concern people as much as in the past. As a consequence, reflection on faith has been marginalized. Furthermore, the natural sense of justice and concern for one's loved ones, who were known to have manifested little faith, has led many to reject the idea that a distant salvation may be refused to them for the sole reason that they did not believe. By this reasoning, a basic fact about faith is not taken into account—namely, that faith is given by God above all as a tool that enables contact with Him, and that it has the capacity to transcend the metaphysical chasm between creature and Creator, between nature and the supernatural.

When we live out faith in a given moment, it is a sort of first installment of eternal life. It sets the encounter with God in motion. Belief in God and, even more, belief *toward* God establishes a point of contact between the soul and God. As a result, the individual becomes susceptible to further impulses of grace and may react to them at will. Thus, there is friendly exchange with God, Who is let into all the dimensions of personal life. Salvific engagement with God begins here on earth. Faith is a divine reality, but one that takes place now. In Heaven, where there is a direct vision of God, faith is no longer necessary. Furthermore, through hope, faith leads to supernatural love that, in turn, conditions faith itself. Charity, which is also a divine reality taking place on earth, will have its sequel in Heaven. Whoever believes toward God through faith formed by charity already has one leg in Heaven. This is because loving people in view of God is living out supernatural love, something that is truly heavenly. Salvation begins on earth, and faith is necessary for its ignition.

When it is understood that faith is a divine gift, one that is to be used and that obviously entails responsibilities, the question of those who have not received the gift, or who have failed to notice it within them and have not developed it, ceases to be so acute. It is more a question about the misfortune of those who have not been given faith, or who have failed to notice received faith, or who have ignored or even poisoned it, rather than the question of their possible moral fault and, therefore, whether they deserve some kind of punishment.

Viewing the issue from the angle of misfortune, rather than of justice or injustice, does not mean that the problem of the salvation of those who do not have faith disappears. It remains intriguing, just as is the case of those who have received the grace of faith, but have not developed it or have willfully rejected, or even ridiculed it. As these questions are addressed, we need to remember that believers should be grateful for the received gift and be faithful toward it. We should not be proud of a gift that, after all, was given gratuitously. And so, also, we should not look down on, judge, or easily sentence those who may not have received faith, or received less, or turned out to be unfaithful to what was given them.

As we ponder these issues, it is good to remember the words of St. Paul about the election of the Jews, which can be applied also to the mysterious and gratuitous grace of faith, given by God at will. Divine gifts are completely free, and so they cannot be seen as a reward, as a punishment, or as deserved. Take the case of the twins, Isaac and Esau. It is not known which one was conceived first and therefore who had the right of precedence. "Before her twin children were born and before either had done good or evil ... in order to stress that God's choice is free, since it depends on the one who calls, not on human merit, Rebecca was told: the elder shall serve the younger" (Rom. 9:11–12). This provokes an immediate question to which a quick answer is given: "Does it follow that God is unjust? Of course not!" (Rom. 9:14). In the grace of faith that enables an encounter with God, just as in the election, "the only thing that counts is not what human beings want or try to do, but the mercy of God" (Rom. 9:16). This again sparks a reaction: "In that case, how can God ever blame anyone?" (Rom. 9:19). St. Paul answers: "But what right have you, a human being, to cross-examine God? The pot has no right to say to the potter: Why did you make me this shape?" (Rom. 9:20). And further on: "If you still hold firm, it is only thanks to your faith. Rather than making you proud, that should make you afraid" (Rom. 11:20). Thus, whoever has received the grace of faith should persevere in it, being thankful that it allows for the engagement with God, without telling God how He should grant His gifts and insisting that He should follow a purely human understanding of justice.

The deepening of the union with God requires a faith that is increasingly pure, with no personal ideas imposed upon Him, telling Him how things ought to be. This is what the two sons from the parable of the merciful Father did (Luke 15:11–32) and what the original Adam had done (Gen. 3:1–7). We need to live in the face of God in gratitude, trust, and hope, receiving His gifts as being totally undeserved, remembering the Father's words addressed to us: "My son, you are with me always and all I have is yours" (Luke 15:31). Similarly, Jesus could say to the Father: "All I have is yours and all you have is mine" (John 17:10).

Hidden faith

How are we then to interpret the situation of those who seem to be totally beyond Christian faith? We can ponder their condition so long as we do not exclude the divine mystery by stubbornly grasping some privately invented means of salvation, or by rejecting a humble and grateful submission to the justification that comes from God (see Rom. 10:3). The question as to whether peoples who have never been evangelized have a chance of salvation is intriguing. Even more so we are perplexed by the dilemma of the eternal happiness of our loved ones who left this world without Baptism, who were without a visible faith, or who even were in conflict with God, having rejected the faith that they had once received.

The author of the Letter to the Hebrews stated clearly: "Now it is impossible to please God without faith, since anyone who comes to Him must believe that He exists and rewards those who try to find Him" (Heb. 11:6). Then, on the basis of his knowledge of history, which was primarily biblical, the writer listed a number of Old Testament figures who directed their faith toward God. Among them he mentioned not only members of the chosen people but also pagans who had believed in God, such as Noah and the prostitute Rahab (Heb. 11:7, 31). All these believers, Jews and pagans, unknowingly were focused upon Christ, even though they did not know His name. Moses, for example, "considered that the insults offered to the Anointed [Christ] were something more precious than all the treasures of Egypt, because he had his eyes fixed on the reward" (Heb. 11:26).

The Scriptures mention several other figures of the pagan world, such as Job, the people of Nineveh, and the Queen of Saba (Matt. 12:41–42), who are treated as saints because of their faith, even though it was located within a natural religiosity. Job's story shows the depth of his faith, unaffected by the deforming suggestions of his family and friends. When his wife urged him to curse God, he replied: "If we take happiness from God's hand, must we not take sorrow too?" (Job 2:10). And when finally he went through the purification forced by suffering, he mumbled initially something incomprehensible and then at the end he confessed to God: "I knew you then only by hearsay; but now, having seen you with my own eyes, I retract all that I have said" (Job 42:5).

In his trial Job recognized the proximity of God, touched by faith, even though he had never been given the message of revelation. Revealed teaching, therefore, clearly states that a true grace of faith, focused on God, is given at times to those who have not been taught the content of faith. Such a grace of faith is located then implicitly within a natural religiosity. It affirms only the existence of God and the fact that He rewards those who trust in His providence. But nevertheless, it is a true, supernatural faith leading toward the Savior. It is subject to deepening and purification, even though those who believe in such a way have never known the name of Jesus and have not received the sacraments. These people are set toward the Mystical Body of Christ and, so in some way, belong to the Church that they have never heard of.[67]

The Catholic Church has always confessed the truth about the possibility of salvation for those who have a true faith deriving from God (even though it may be poor in content and enveloped within a natural religiosity) and who live according to that faith. This is irrespective of whether such people were born before Christ or after Him, whether they belong to the chosen people or lived centuries ago in distant Australia or pagan Peru. If they believe in the existence of God and His providence, counting on it and directing their trustful faith toward Him, then they have a part in the salvation that Christ merited in the Redemption. If they are saved, they are saved by the grace of Christ and not by the grace of some Buddha, Krishna, or Allah.

Contemporary knowledge of history and geography has expanded our horizon of time and space. But the Church's answer to the question of the salvation of people having a true, but content-poor, faith has been same over the centuries.[68] We are saved

[67] Pius XII, in his encyclical *Mystici corporis Christi*, mentions those, who *etiamsi inscio quodam desiderio ac voto ad mysticum Redemptoris Corpus ordinentur* (by an unconscious desire and longing ... have a certain relationship with the Mystical Body of the Redeemer). Denzinger and Schönmetzer, *Enchiridion Symbolorum* 3821.

[68] St. Thomas Aquinas, *Summa Theologiae* Ia-IIae, q. 106, art. 1 ad. 3; art. 3, ad. 2; II Vatican Council, *Decree on the Mission Activity of the*

through faith that we receive from God when we live it out. But since divine gifts are unequal, there is a greater chance of engaging with God among those who not only have faith, but also can focus it, thanks to the teaching derived from revelation, passed on to them by the Church, and nourish it with the sacraments. Such people also have a greater duty with respect to their faith. They should not proudly attribute merit to themselves for the Christian faith that they possess, nor dismiss those who have received less nourishment for their fragile, hidden, but true faith. Undoubtedly the gifts that flow from the Paschal Mystery of Jesus—that is, the sacraments of the Church—are an extraordinary food for faith. One is to receive them with gratitude, while also believing that those who have not been given the chance to hear the name of Christ, but in some vague way focus upon Him, "are all heroes of the faith, but they did not receive what was promised, since God had made provision for us to have something better, and they were not to reach perfection except with us" (Heb. 11:39–40). The salutary union with God is varied, differing according to the gifts that individuals have received and their response to them. God has tied the granting of graces with the sacraments, but He Himself is not bound by them. And so in His good pleasure He may grant gifts as He wills, even outside the visible, sacramental structure of the Church. Each person should therefore be grateful for the received gifts, responding truly in love of God for these proofs of His love.

Can we then draw the conclusion that all, including those who declare themselves to be unbelievers and those who hold the beliefs

---

Church "Ad gentes," no 7: "Therefore though God in ways known to Himself can lead those inculpably ignorant of the Gospel to find that faith without which it is impossible to please Him (Heb. 11:6), yet a necessity lies upon the Church (1 Cor. 9:16), and at the same time a sacred duty, to preach the Gospel."

of any conceivable natural religion, have the divine grace of faith automatically, and that they also had it in the past? Is it not basically irrelevant whether one consciously belongs to the Church or not, because all are Christians anyway, though some are aware of this and others are unaware, being "anonymous" Christians? And so does the difference consist only in the possessed knowledge about the possibility of maintaining a relationship with God? Such conclusions are erroneous, and for a number of reasons.

First of all, grace is not to be treated as being due to us. Were it to be given automatically and equally to all, it would be a part of nature and not a new and specific divine gift. The means to transcend the chasm between creature and Creator is not natural. It is a pure and additional gift of God, given according to the measure of His generosity. There is nothing in nature that enables a personal union with the Creator. When faith in the living God appears in the human heart, it is something essentially new, different from the natural inclinations, including the natural curiosity about the source and end of all being. Faith is a grace. It is given by God, so that an encounter between Him and the individual can take place. Faith sets the supernatural life in the soul in motion.

The fact that faith appears in the soul is a pure gift of God, given in His sweeping gesture. A conscious response resulting from that faith deepens the encounter with God and disposes one for the reception of further gifts. Since gratitude may refer to the initial gift, or to the further developed and richer gifts flowing from an ongoing intimacy of the soul with God, it follows that there is diversity in the levels of gift. This should not be a cause for indignation, pride, or judgment, in line with human criteria of justice. Rather, this only discloses the mysterious generosity of the divine heart. In fact, there is nothing surprising in this. We observe something similar in human relationships. Some have a deeper love, and others are more cold and indifferent in their relationships. Why should the interpersonal relationship between God and humans be different, since God treats everyone as a unique individual? We certainly know that God is just and merciful, because this has been revealed to us. We also know that He "wants everyone to be saved" (1 Tim. 2:4). But how this works out in the case of individuals is not something for us to assess.

Second, we need to remember that the faith of those who have received the grace of faith but do not have the Word of God and the sacraments of the Church is endangered and may be distorted. When faith is not nourished, developed, and purified, it may easily turn into proud fundamentalism, an aggressive religiosity. It may become entangled in some purely human projects and ideologies. Or it may become extinguished in the soul or expelled by sin that rejects God. This danger threatens not only those who have received faith alone, without the Word of God and the Church. Those who have been brought to the Church through Baptism and have received a Christian formation are also at risk. Christians, too, lose their faith, distort it, and kill the charity that forms the faith. This comes about through certain sins that, precisely for this reason, are described as mortal. But certainly those who have received faith with no revelation and no contact with the Church are more exposed to the danger of deforming their faith or losing it.

The possibility of an "anonymous" faith within a purely natural religiosity should not be imagined so generously such that one dismisses the nourishment for faith—the Word and the sacraments—and forgets Jesus' precept: "Go out to the whole world; proclaim the Good News to all creation. He who believes and is baptized will be saved; he who does not believe will be condemned" (Mark 16:15–16). The Church has to preach the Gospel to all nations and to administer the sacraments, because this is Jesus' command. He said: "I am the good shepherd; I know my own and my own know me, just as the Father knows me and I know the Father.... And there are other sheep I have that are not of this fold, and these I have to lead as well. They too will listen to my voice, and there will be only one flock, and one shepherd" (John 10:14–16).

There are people who have a very hazy relationship with the Savior, one smothered by erroneous views and fancies and by an undemanding, even debasing, ethics. If there is a hidden implicit faith in them, it is meager. Jesus wants to be known personally, not only through some nebulous presentiment about divine providence in which there is some perspective of redemption, with no notions, words, and signs expressing it. Jesus wants our human connection with Him to be up to the standard of His relationship with the Father. We are called to a divine filiation. As adopted children of God we can relate to our heavenly Father together with our Brother Jesus. Only when all people know Jesus through an intimate spiritual bond that is made possible by faith and charity will they know Him in a way that is comparable to the way in which Jesus is known by the heavenly Father. It is then that there will be one fold and one shepherd.

From the mere fact that divine generosity extends also to those who have not heard the words of the Gospel and have no chance of receiving the sacraments of the Church, it does not follow that we can be satisfied with the status of an "anonymous" Christian. The lack of the fullness of faith is always a misfortune. In the case of many, this is not culpable. But there are those who have received a true faith, and yet that they have not developed it or even have rejected it. We should not readily move from reflecting on the possibility of Neanderthals having the grace of faith to simply exempting ourselves from a needed concern for the faith, or to childishly consoling those who have received the Christian faith and then lost it.

Those who have received the grace of faith should be concerned about it, develop it, and ensure that it grows. It is true that there may be individuals who, for various reasons, declare themselves to be unbelievers, particularly if they have been raised in an environment that is unfriendly toward faith, and yet the grace of faith persists in them, prompting them from time to time to trust in God and to express love for Him. Conversely, there are also those who declare their faith, including even members of the Church's clergy, and yet in practice they do not tend to it and, in difficult or happy moments, do not relate to God. The observation of the faithful who refer to a particular priest but not to another as "a man of faith" shows that even bystanders somehow sense who is relating to God and who is only wearing a pious mask without a true living faith. Such observations and reflections about a hidden or weak faith, however, cannot be raised to the rank of a basic theological principle that would allow doubts about the role of a living faith and the importance and value of a conscious and active belonging to the Church.

Faith has to be nourished by the Word of God, the sacraments, and participation in the community of believing members of the Church. We do not have an angelic nature, and so we need physical contact with believers and sacramental signs. We do not live in Heaven, in which the visible structure of the Church will no longer be necessary. The conscious focusing of faith toward Christ—who is not only grasped in some nebulous way, but, thanks to the Incarnation and the Gospel records, is imaginable and knowable—and the opening of the soul through the reception of the sacraments to the graces of the Redemption won by Him and, also, persistence in the Church community, are a great blessing for faith.

It is true that some people have had no chance to learn about Christ and no occasion to receive the sacraments. This should therefore impel the Church faithful to find a resolution. That is why, in essence, the Church is not only sacramental, but also missionary. Both dimensions should not be dismissed in the name of an excessively generous expansion of the undoubted possibility of salvation for those who, through no fault of their own, have minimal contact with the Church.[69] We need not forget that there have been, and continue to be, those who have had an occasion to know Jesus and yet have not followed Him. We should not limit ourselves to consoling them with the idea that in their unbelief they may still find some crumbs of the salutary faith, but, instead, we should show them the perspective of living the faith in its plenitude.

The issue of a hidden, salvific faith is tied with the problem of the fate of infants who have died without Baptism. The Church has been struggling with this question for centuries. Theologians have come up with a place called Limbo, which, viewed from Heaven, seems to be not like Heaven, but which, viewed from Hell, seems to be Heaven. The Church has never formally made a pronouncement on this issue. Undoubtedly the gift of faith requires that it be set in motion through acts of faith, spiritual moments undertaken in view of God. The quality of the interpersonal encounter with God taking place here on earth conditions the intimacy with Him. An

[69] Karl Rahner, it seems, who extensively developed the theme of anonymous Christians, has gone too far in his conjectures. He tried to find some exit for those who have heard the evangelical preaching and then reject or ignore it. His reasoning boils down to the claim that explicit acceptance of the truths of faith proclaimed by the Church is of secondary importance. Such a view questions the role of the glorified humanity of Jesus as the object of salutary faith and weakens the meaningfulness of the visible, sacramental structure of the Church. In a sort of "imperialistic" way, it attributes a salvific meaning to every nebulous presentiment or to all manifestations of any religiosity whatever, which automatically and "anonymously" are treated as Christian. See Dulles, *The Assurance of Things Hoped For*, pp. 152–153, 173.

infant whose spiritual faculties are as yet undeveloped has limited possibilities for making acts of faith and growing in faith and charity, though, of course, we have to remember that a pure entrustment of the self to God is easier for a child than an adult. God receives great glory from the poor in spirit, and so also from little children. But can this be said also about infants, who do not yet have a reason because they are still in their mothers' wombs, or about embryos locked in refrigerators?

There are many questions for which we have no answers. And we should not offer false responses. In the face of such questions that at times are very painful, it is better to invite one to persist in trustful openness toward the divine mystery. The *Catechism of the Catholic Church* only states that "the great mercy of God … and Jesus' tenderness toward children … allow us to hope that there is a way of salvation for children who have died without baptism" (1261).

Resistances against faith

There are sins against the moral order. They harm others and the sinner himself who, as a result, is morally weakened. Sins against justice encroach upon the rights of others. Sins against internal resourcefulness, known traditionally as prudence, impede one's ability to pull oneself together and to do what the conscience indicates. Sins against temperance and fortitude weaken self-control, and this often leads to a lack of respect for the dignity and rights of others.

Sins that cut down, or abolish, the bond with God are of a distinct species. They concern the theological order, which, in essence, is delicate and fragile but also strong by the force of grace, and so they often escape attention. But they are dangerous for both the spiritual life and the moral life. It is through supernatural faith and charity that the dynamics of divine life are sparked. Only when this divine life is present in the soul can the believer find supernatural power that enables him to live in truth and to react courageously to moral challenges. The relationship with God, upheld by faith and charity, which set grace in motion, introduces grace into the realm of thinking, deciding, and feeling. Without trusting in grace, dealing with weaknesses and various types of temptations becomes extremely difficult, as does engaging in works of charity that bring something of God's kingdom to the world. Such is the teaching of Jesus: "Cut off from me you can do nothing" (John 15:5). Understanding this particular "psychology" of divine life, and eventual resistances against grace, is essential for the vibrancy of the spiritual life.

Every grave sin destroys the supernatural life in the soul and, precisely for this reason, it is called mortal. To return to a lively encounter with God we need a new gift of grace. Mortal sin, however, does not kill faith. Faith persists after sin and is an aid in the renewed return to God. This means that those who are entangled in sins, and for this reason do not receive the sacraments, are still Christians, on the condition that they have not renounced faith: They belong to the Church. Only sins that directly contradict faith destroy it in the soul, causing a break with God. That is why infidelity—the rejection of faith—wounds the spiritual life more deeply than sins against chastity or justice, and so it is the most serious sin.

Infidelity at times is coupled with regard for great human values. There are, after all, people who serve others altruistically in the name of ideologies that they espouse, and yet they reject faith. Clarity in human sciences often enjoys a greater esteem than the obscurity of faith. A scientist dressed in his white overalls spontaneously generates intellectual respect. But to accept the words of a bishop who, with a miter on his head, speaks in the name of

God, faith is required. And that faith can be difficult. The message of faith is passed on in the Church by individuals who do not necessarily inspire admiration for their erudition or manifest some higher moral ethos. And so the recognition that faith has greater value than the achievements of culture often seems scandalous to the mind.

The obstinacy of infidelity has multiple forms. At times, it is a rigid hardening of the heart or an outraged autonomy of the mind that proudly insists upon its intellectual freedom. Pride that rejects dependency on God is the greatest enemy of the life of grace. Yet it may be tied with natural honesty and generosity. But just as in faith there is the free reception of revealed truth by the intellect that respects the authority of the revealing God so, similarly, with infidelity there is an act of the intellect under the influence of the will in which truth is rejected. This is not necessarily the result of a *conscious* ill will. It is something that we cannot assess in others, because we do not know their consciences.

When infidelity is consciously maintained, it has an impact on the intellectual life—but it does not completely overwhelm it, because a worldview that excludes faith does not always cover the entire cognitive sphere. However, since it kills the life of grace, infidelity has a negative impact on the moral life.

Infidelity, just like faith, may be sure, or it may be coupled with doubts that put a brake on judgment. It may manifest itself by stopping short at a particular point in the understanding of faith and a refusal to reach out deeper into the divine mystery. It may pick and choose among the truths of faith, following its own criteria, meaning that the basic motive of faith has been vitiated. This happens when personal reasons are held higher than the authority of God and of the Church, which teaches in His name. There are people who accept the faith of their childhood but protest when the Church proclaims deeper truths of faith because they judge that they are not fitting for them. Here there is a resistance against the grace of the Holy Spirit, whereas it is He who leads, deepens, and purifies faith.

Heresy consists in a conscious denial of one or several specific truths of faith while simultaneously retaining others. In it the basic motive of faith is rejected. Heresy differs from error in faith, which may be the result of a failure to learn the truths or of not having had an occasion to acquire a precise knowledge of the contents of faith. In formal heresy, there is a conscious erection of one's own reasons above the reception of the truth of faith. This blocks trust toward God, which is why heresy harms the life of grace. It is not so important whether it questions a major truth of faith or a minor one, because in itself it distorts the relationship toward God. Heresy, of course, concerns only authentic truths of faith and not scientific or even theological opinions about issues that have not been explicitly defined by the Church. We need to ponder the truths of faith, and that is why within faith there is room for the penetration of its contents. Accordingly, diverse views may be formulated, so long as they do not contradict the basic truths.

In heresy, the decisive role is played by personal opinion, and so the motive of faith is no longer the acceptance of truth because it is transmitted by the Church. That is why heresies generate quarrels. When infidelity and some of its forms, like heresy and apostasy, are spoken of, more than anything, what is meant is an internal disposition of the heart that opposes truth, and not some sociological group. Many people belong to Christian denominations that broke off from the Church centuries ago, and so the faith they confess lacks fullness or, on some point, is erroneous. But this does not necessarily mean that they have sinned in rejecting faith. Positive infidelity that is a conscious willed rejection of faith is one thing, and the misfortune of not having faith or of having it in an imprecise way is another.

Apostasy is a direct form of infidelity that consists in the rejection of faith by somebody who had faith. Apostasy differs from paganism because pagans express respect for God in a natural way as they understand Him. Apostates reject God directly. This means that the apostate puts himself in the center, around which everything else is to rotate. Since apostasy is the opposite of faith, it is willed—but people often lack consistency. A rebellious teenager sometimes expresses infidelity verbally, but at a deeper level continues to believe. Thus, apostasy should not be easily judged. There are people who say that they are atheists, and yet faith continues to linger in their souls, in particular if they were baptized, even though they are not aware of this. In time there comes a moment when faith awakens in them. Even forthright declarations of apostasy cannot repeal divine gifts. There are cases in which apostates seeking notoriety demand that information about their baptism be deleted from parochial records. Such a purely bureaucratic measure cannot stop God from encompassing an individual with His love, because He "never takes back His gifts or revokes His choice" (Rom. 11:29).

Heresy and apostasy erect an internal spiritual barrier against faith, whereas the inverse of the confession of faith is blasphemy, the pronouncement of words against God. Blasphemy is not infidelity, because the blasphemer believes in the existence of God and speaks out against Him consciously in a provocative, scandalous way, finding enjoyment in this. Blasphemy is something more than making fun of religiosity or "offending religious feelings," because it attacks God directly. Someone may not like some culturally conditioned forms of religion and pastoral initiatives. There is nothing wrong in this. But the blasphemer insults God instead of confessing faith in Him. Some blasphemers irritate believers by playing with religious symbols, thereby generating a social scandal that they provocatively incite. Sometimes individuals repetitively use swear words that have a religious connotation, or experience blasphemous flashes of imagination. These are signs of a sensitive disorder or emotional stress and not blasphemy, which is a sin of the intellect. True blasphemy insults faith directly, and so it prevents an encounter with God. As such, it is a serious sin.

Traditionally, some sins are said to be against the Holy Spirit. They not only destroy the order of grace in the soul, which is the consequence of every mortal sin, but also erect a barrier against it, as a result of which grace cannot be reborn. So long as these sins persist in the heart, the sinner shields himself against God and closes in on himself. That is why these sins are like a foretaste of Hell, where God is absent. They include despair, presumptuous sinning with a simultaneous conviction that grace is deserved anyway, impenitence, obduracy in sin, the rejection of a known truth, and envy of grace in others. In despair, the sinner believes that God may save others, but not him.

The tradition of antiquity observed that gluttony, drunkenness, and sins against chastity result in the darkening of the mind and the weakening of spiritual perception. These sins stand in opposition to two gifts of the Holy Spirit, understanding and knowledge, which deepen faith. One who believes truly and deeply is sensitive to divine signals that urge toward greater generosity, charity, and responsibility. But the one who prefers superficiality ceases to sense the ways of God and often reacts to coming purifications and crises with aggression, protest, and accusations against others. Persistence in faith acknowledges divine care also in moments of difficulty during the pilgrimage of life. One who lacks a lively faith rebels against God on such occasions, and then the heart becomes hard and stony (see Ps. 95:8).

When one tries to decipher possible barriers that destroy faith or block its growth, a glance at the great religions of the world is illuminating. The question here is not whether, or to what extent, grace enabling belief in the existence of God and in His providence, which is minimally necessary for salvation, appears within non-Christian religions but, rather, how this divine gift may be seriously imperiled by possible distortions. All religions have some kernel of truth, but there are also serious errors. So, if those who belong to them receive the grace of faith from God—of course, not through the rites of their religion, but independently of it—then that grace, enveloped within a non-Christian religiosity, finds itself in a context that does not nourish it; therefore, it may be easily deformed. The identification of the typical characteristics of various religions may facilitate the recognition of hidden resistances that sometimes come about also within Christian faith, and prevent its flowering in the soul.

A basically heretical attitude may be espoused without formally leaving the Catholic Church. The essence of heresy consists in the replacement of the basic motive of faith—the authority of the self-revealing God—with some other personal reason. Those who pick and choose amongst the truths of faith and moral teachings, rejecting what is found to be unsuitable, irrespective of whether this is done from a liberal or an excessively traditionalist position, essentially adopt a heretical approach. This wounds the Church by introducing a division and, what is more, it poisons the internal readiness to be led by God.

Someone else may adopt an attitude that is typical among Jews and Muslims who reject Christ. A faith that is initially on track may stop short at a given point, with internal resistances preventing it from going further toward the divine mystery. Basically, the Jewish and Muslim outlook imposes a brake, an unwillingness to accept the novelty of the New Testament due to the conviction that it is unbecoming for God to go so far, up to the point where, in His mercy, He takes human sin on His shoulders and frees us from it. By this mentality, what seems to be decisive is holding on to law and justice and the ensuing order. The adventure of relating to God through faith and charity seems so nebulous and enigmatic that thinking about it is banned. This is the attitude of the older brother of the prodigal son, who argued with his father and insisted on his own way of seeing things, not wanting to take part in the celebration of mercy.

Another type of infidelity is analogous to Buddhism. Some Christians treat the dogmas of faith as being completely irrelevant because what counts, they claim, is not the reception of some blurry truth, but only personal, subjective psychic states. For them, their own experience is most important. They sometimes describe it as mystical because it gives them a sense of peace and allows for concentration on self and indifference toward others. Such delight in oneself, in one's own psyche and mental states, may generate a sense of superiority over other people who are moved by certain matters, challenges, and emotions. Of course, this is not true mysticism, and the Gospel does not lead to this.

There are others who are so fascinated with tolerance that they deny the possibility of knowing any truth whatsoever. It seems to them that Christianity cannot insist upon nonnegotiable truths because, according to them, religion ultimately has to reconcile everything with everything. So, if one has to affirm Christ, this may be done, they say, but the notion of His unique role in the history of salvation is unacceptable, because this is intolerant toward others. Therefore, all religions are considered to be identical, being merely a local cultural expression of the same. Those with such an approach, which is typical for Hinduism, are willing to accept every thesis and every hero as a part of a pantheon of multiple deities. For them it is unimportant whether these are Hindu gods, Christ, ideological political leaders, or idols of music, sports, religion, or philosophy. They are all recognized and respected—and treated as being basically irrelevant. Such a fusion of everything with everything in some unity in the name of universal tolerance may influence thinking, and may go hand in hand with external gestures of Christian religiosity. This, however, is fundamentally contrary to Christianity because it is a form of infidelity that poisons salvific faith.

Concern about the quality of faith—about precision in its formulation and that it be truly alive and pure—elicited internally and focused directly on God, is fundamental. True faith enables union with God and openness to His grace. If the expression of faith is erroneous; if its motive is wrong; or if the striving toward God is derailed, then the spiritual life declines. Any eventual good that is subsequently done has a natural value, but its execution is more difficult because it lacks divine support. The hidden divine dynamism that enables human acts to be enriched by the fecundity of God Himself is missing.

The preaching of faith

Faith is an unmerited gift of grace that sets the spiritual life in motion. But the subject matter of that faith, which focuses thinking within it and consequently influences action dependent on God, is received from the Church. It is essential, therefore, that teaching based on the apostolic message be passed on. But the person teaching faith must remember that the preaching role is only ministerial. The supernatural life is never *granted* by the speaker but comes directly from God. Just as a mother does not give life, but only transmits it, so the ministry of a preacher may assist in the moment, when faith is born in the unbeliever, but that life of grace is given by God.

Most often, teachers of faith are not dealing with true pagans or absolute atheists. Rather, they face those who have been touched by the grace of faith. If their listeners were baptized, they already have received the seeds of the supernatural life, even if it happened in infancy and their faith has not grown. But even if the speaker addresses the unbaptized, often, before the meeting, the Holy Spirit has already been at work and touched these unbaptized hearts, awakening some orientation toward God due to which they are willing to hear the word of faith at least minimally. Since words themselves do not produce faith in the hearers, the speaker should avoid pride and should not attribute gloriously to oneself the capacity to elicit faith in others. The preacher's or catechist's ministry is more modest: It is to announce the message of faith received in revelation and handed down in the Church, counting on the work of God Himself in this process. The subject matter that is taught nourishes, strengthens, and defends the faith that already exists in souls and comes from God. The preacher presents truths so as to expand faith and to safeguard it from deformations, thereby allowing it to grow. As divine grace is called in by faith, it reaches all dimensions of life—the intellectual life, the sphere of personal decisions, and the emotional life that needs to be focused. What disposition, then, should the speaker have so that faith grows in human hearts?

The one who is preaching faith needs to be constantly aware that, in essence, it is a divine reality. Its supernatural quality is not an incidental, but a basic characteristic. Faith is a gift given by God, enabling communication with Him. The object of faith, and its fundamental motive, and also its internal dynamic are from God. Since faith derives from God and leads to Him, its source of growth is in Him. It is true that the reason also functions beyond faith, and that is why occasionally it raises questions about faith's credibility and wonders whether it is prudent to allow oneself to be drawn into the adventure of engaging with God. But ultimately the adherence to God in faith is not based on these external, prudential, and apologetic musings of reason. Faith finds its justification within itself. When we believe, we move to the supernatural order of grace, based on the self-communicating God. Then, in our own human thinking, we attribute primacy to the knowledge of God Himself, and in our limited human love in all its dimensions we cede priority to the dynamics of divine love.

Whoever transmits the truths of faith has to be constantly aware that it is faith that enables the soul's contact with God. The preacher has to believe in the supernatural character of the confessed faith, and so also believe in the presence of the grace of the Holy Spirit in the souls of both the speaker and those listening. Since contact with God through faith triggers an immediate effusion of the invisible but real divine grace (as in the case of the sick woman who touched the hem of Jesus' cloak with her finger and His heart with her faith), the preacher has to believe that internal faith, elicited precisely at the moment the words are said, brings down grace from Heaven. This is essential in the liturgy and while teaching from the altar, but also in every catechesis, in conversations that aim at the strengthening of faith, in family dialogues around the table, in conversations with strangers, in writing books, and in speaking to the media. In all these moments, calling upon a lively faith ensures the spiritual force and fruitfulness of the expressed word. The astounding power of the ministry of the word of St. John Paul II did not flow from his theatrical experience or his command of languages, but from the quality of his prayer that accompanied his words.[70]

Often in human contacts, in particular when we deal with difficult issues requiring spiritual receptivity, we encounter resistance.

[70] I was shown in the Polish College in Rome some Xerox copies of the conferences St. John Paul II preached during his early Wednesday audiences. He wrote them by hand. Instead of numbering the pages, on the top of each sheet he wrote the verses of the hymn to the Holy Spirit. This means that as he was preparing these discourses, he was calling by faith the assistance of the Paraclete.

This experience of spiritual poverty, of the awkwardness of one's own word, and of an aversion against the spoken truth, is extremely precious because it forces one to call upon the grace of the Holy Spirit. If, instead of an act of faith, there is an outburst of anger at the interlocutor or a search for rational, supposedly convincing arguments that are external to faith, then there is no understanding. But if in the helplessness of spiritual poverty we invite in the grace of God, then some simple, seemingly banal words that have already been heard by the other in the past may be said that, this time, penetrate the soul. A true apostolate participates in the Paschal Mystery of Jesus. Whoever has been sent by the Church to serve and to preach, even though they feel they lack force, talent, moral perfection, knowledge, and human charm that could attract others, should believe in God and call Him by faith precisely during their ministry. The speaker then becomes transparent to divine power.

What is decisive for the life of faith is not the magnitude or quantity of pastoral events, but the faith of the participants and the quality of their adherence to God. Whenever the supernatural genesis of faith in the soul, and its internal divine power that enables its growth, have been forgotten, this has led to an improper rift in thinking about faith. Faith was then pushed to the level of emotional, sentimental experiences and reason was locked in skepticism.

Pastors sometimes think that generally they have to offer pleasant religious sensations to the faithful, and when they are talking to the educated, they feel obliged to excise faith and move to a purely rational discourse that presupposes that God does not exist. They try to impress intellectuals with a philosophical lecture slipping often into sociology or politics, which is divisive; meanwhile the masses are given only religious experiences. A liturgical setting, with its artistic beauty and communal feelings generated by a compact mass of people animated by the same collective atmosphere, may give lofty and joyful moments. Such shared happenings can be very exciting, deeply marking the imagination and emotions. But they are not necessarily a sign of a lively faith, a willingness to compose oneself and set out toward God with the conviction that it is possible to base oneself on obscure, ineffable, but real grace. But this is what St. Peter did as he walked on water. He moved forward in seeming insecurity but on a path that was certain, thanks to the power of God.

True faith activates charity, forgiveness, generosity, courage in undertaking that which is difficult, and the gift of self, above all in view of God, and sometimes for no other reason than that. Collective elation provides an easy satisfaction, a moment of enchantment, a feeling of strength in the face of enemies, but it does not necessarily bring one closer to God. Participation in massive liturgical or prayer events, particularly when they are adorned by self-advertising flags and banners with no religious message, may be enticing. It is analogous to the frenzy of football matches or rock concerts, though liturgical events carry a more serious weight. Attending large prayer gatherings does not necessarily entail a real willingness to live in accord with faith, nor does it necessarily deepen it. When pastoral events are assessed not on the basic criterion of whether they truly deepen the supernatural life in the souls but solely by their size, then in a country where people can be easily invited to such spectacular ceremonies, social applause is quick. But what is the point? What is better: the true leading of one person toward sanctity—toward God—or the sprinkling of large crowds with holy water?

As we ponder this, it is good to note the example of Jesus. He did not shirk from massive gatherings, but He had no great expectations about them. The Gospel recalls one such "happening" organized by Jesus. When He fed the crowds, they were so delighted that they held Him to be a prophet and wanted to call Him a king (John 6:14–15). Jesus then withdrew for prayer, and when they found Him again, He spoke in a mysterious language that required faith to comprehend. Jesus was not bothered by the fact that they did not understand His words and murmured against Him. He inflexibly held on to His theme, which was beyond the comprehension of rational minds. What is more, His words were harsh, provocative, and accusing: "You can see me and still you do not believe!" (John 6:36). He demanded that His audience be guided by faith that comes from God: "No one can come to me unless he is drawn by the Father who sent me" (John 6:44). He wanted them to accept that which reason rebels against: "Anyone who does eat my flesh and drink my blood has eternal life" (John 6:54). In this there was no ingratiation, no adapting to their skepticism and subjective expectations, or to notions of their culture, no searching for applause or fear that the crowd would dwindle in size. And when "many of his disciples left Him and stopped going with Him" (John 6:66), Jesus continued to provoke the remaining handful: "What about you, do you want to go away too?" (John 6:67). And then Peter confessed his faith: "Lord, who shall we go to? You have the message of eternal life, and we believe; we know that you are the Holy One of God" (John 6:68–69). Peter spoke in his own name and in the name of the apostles, but not all of them persevered in faith, because "one of the Twelve . . . was going to betray him" (John 6:71).

Preaching faith consists in focusing minds drawn internally by the Father to the revealed, but obscure, mystery—that is, toward the living God. That is why reason often protests against this. Nevertheless, faith needs to be preached courageously, going beyond the natural limits of the mind that desires clarity. Whoever truly does this, irrespective of whether he is a preaching bishop, a teacher, or a parent educating a child, is doing something of huge significance, because when minds are opened by faith, space for the working of divine grace is extended.

We speak of God not only when we discuss profound dogmas of faith, but also when we address moral issues. Christian moral teaching is about God, Who inhabits human hearts by grace and transforms them from within, eliciting acts of charity that are fruitful with the love of God Himself. Therefore, a discourse on faith should not be limited to the psychology of the act of faith, to the sociology of religion, or even to resistances against faith. It needs to be stressed that faith is above all the entry of God into the life of the human mind, which recognizes Him as the basic object of its cognition, the First Truth from which further consequences in the spiritual and moral life derive. God adapts Himself to the human mind in such a way that it may adhere to Him in faith and open up to the entire dynamism of His life.

It follows, therefore, that the purity of faith—focused directly upon God without being caught on incidental or ideological issues that sometimes are intertwined with faith—and its precision are crucial. Faith is of greater value than the moral virtues, because they are based upon it. It is also greater than the achievements of science and culture. Since faith ensures contact with God, there should be no tinkering in the transmission. Faith opens up to the mystery of God, in view of Him, on the basis of what He has revealed. And it is this divine message that is to be handed down. Precisely for this reason, medieval theologians were very critical of those who deformed faith. They viewed despoiling faith as something worse than the corruption of money through devaluation, or even than the declaration of war against an enemy.

The preacher of faith has a daunting task. He is to direct minds toward the mystery of the living God and to show how, in the context of various moral challenges and duties, it is possible to live by grace received from God. The basic salvific value of faith lies not in the clarity of its message, even though its elucidation is always beneficial, but in its capacity to ensure a contact with God and to set the divine life in motion. A person may possess exact knowledge about the truths of faith, and yet faith may be dead or dormant in him. Growth in faith does not come about through a more precise knowledge of the dogmas of faith, but through a real encounter with the living God. However, a better knowledge of the truths of faith does help. It nourishes faith and defends it against views that may destroy it.

Faith is not just the will to adhere to God. Basically, it is cognition, a supernatural overpowering of the mind by God, the First Truth. Since it locates reason within the revealed Truth, the entire life may then be ordered toward God, the highest and true Good. This means that human life may be measured by reference to that supreme criterion disclosed by God—Jesus Christ, the incarnate Word of the Father. That is why faith may be authentically preached only by the one who believes that Jesus is the basic message to be passed on, and that it is primarily the Father who draws the believer to Him (John 6:44).

It follows therefore that witnessing in faith should not be exaggerated. Jesus said: "You will be my witnesses" (Acts 1:8), and so preachers of faith are to point to the Risen One. Sometimes it is said that people are drawn more by witnesses than by teachers of faith. This needs to be understood correctly. Priests are not to draw attention to themselves. They are not to tell people how good they feel because of their faith. Instead, they are to direct faith toward Christ, in whom there is salvation. A priest needs to witness to Him, even in moments when he painfully experiences some weakness. He is to teach not what he considers to be meaningful, but the full truth that he has received, and which has been handed down in the Church since apostolic times.

When the preacher's faith in the power of faith is weak, the attachment to the living God is also weak. This explains why some priests constantly talk about themselves, their achievements, their experiences, or their difficulties. In doing so, they do not build up the faith of the listeners. Instead they enervate them. And, furthermore, if they do start tutoring them, telling them how they have to behave morally, but at the same time they do not lead them to a deeper faith, then such impossible and frustrating teaching meets with indignation and rejection. Evangelization is truly meaningful and new only when its novelty derives from a fresh impulse of grace coming from the Holy Spirit. This comes about in souls whenever they are opened by true acts of faith reaching out toward the divine mystery. When the novelty of evangelization is due only to some new technique or innovative pastoral strategy, it soon lays bare its superficiality and ends with discouragement.

In searching for an appropriate method of preaching the faith, we may recall the experience of the early Church. The early Christians focused attention on the inner disposition of the priest, vitally influencing the quality and fecundity of his prayer. New historical studies have shown that in the Church of antiquity, in which married men were ordained priests and bishops (by then their children were probably already grown up), from the moment of ordination they were required to refrain from sexual intercourse with their wives.[71] The Synod of Bishops called in Carthage in 390, citing an earlier tradition on this issue that dated from apostolic times, explained the meaning of this requirement. What was at stake was that those who administer the sacraments "would be able to obtain from the Lord what in pure simplicity they are pleading

[71] This is how the Fathers of the Church interpreted the words of the Gospel about the leaving of houses, families, and wives (Matt. 19:27–30; Luke 18:28–30) and the ruling of St. Paul that a priest or bishop has to be chosen from among men who had not been married more than once (Titus 1:6; 1 Tim. 3:2). See St. Jerome, *Commentariorum in epistolam ad Titum* I, vv. 8–9 (*PL* 26, 603b–4°).

for."[72] Chastity helps focus attention toward God, as a result of which faith touches God more directly and, therefore, has greater fecundity. The same can be said about all preaching of faith. The greater the prayerfulness of the preacher and the more that superficial entertainments engaging the psyche are eliminated, the purer is the faith, making the grace of preaching more fruitful.

The person who truly believes and who engages faith in prayer, truly communicating with the divine mystery, not only unites with God, but also passes on the supernatural life, drawing others to that spiritual life. We should remember this particularly while keeping vigil at the side of the dying. Bodily pain concentrates upon self: The one who is suffering is focused on the pain. But, at the same time, the dying person experiences the realization that so many issues that had been so important in life become distant and unimportant. The dying person is left with only one task, and that is being united with God. The purification caused by the distancing of all other issues leaves only this unique and most important matter in life. The question is whether this person dies believing and loving God or not. Those who stand around may sustain the faith of the dying by their prayer. If they truly join to God in faith, their physical presence supports the faith of the one who is passing away, so that his or her faith will not waver or succumb to despair. And then the dying person moves in trust and love toward God.

[72] The Synod of Carthage declared: *Decet sacros antistites ac Dei sacerdotes nec non et levitas vel qui sacramentis divinis inserviunt, continentes esse in omnibus, quo possint simpliciter quod a Domino postulant impetrare, ut quod apostoli docuerunt et ipsa servavit antiquitas, nos quoque custodiamus.... Omnibus placet ut episcopus, presbyter et diaconus, pudicitiae custodes, etiam ab uxoribus se abstineant ut in omnibus et ab omnibus custodiatur qui altario inserviunt.* See *Corpus Christianorum* 149, p. 13, quoted by Fr. Christian Cochini, *Apostolic Origins of Priestly Celibacy* (San Francisco: Ignatius Press, 1990), p. 5.

The Spark of Faith

The preaching of the Gospel to the Jews and pagans is the fulfillment of the mission entrusted to the Church by Jesus: "Go, therefore, make disciples of all nations; baptize them in the name of the Father and of the Son and of the Holy Spirit.... And know that I am with you always; yes, to the end of time" (Matt. 28:19–20). The more universal the preaching of the Gospel is, reaching out to the most distant corners of the earth, the more the Second Coming of the Lord is hastened. Preaching the Gospel to nations that had received the faith and then have fallen away is a different but also necessary task. The apostasy of former Christians does not distance the Second Coming of Jesus: It foretells it. At the end of time "many will fall away ... but the man who stands firm to the end will be saved" (Matt. 24:10, 13). "But when the Son of Man comes, will He find any faith on earth?" (Luke 18:8). Maybe, at the end of time, there will be just a handful of believers in Jesus?

About the Author

Fr. Wojciech Giertych was born in 1951 in London, England, as the son of Polish émigrés. After secondary school, he moved to Poland and studied history at the University of Poznań, where he graduated in 1975. That year he entered the Polish Province of the Dominican Order. He studied philosophy and theology at the Dominican House of Studies in Kraków and was ordained a priest in 1981. From 1981 to 1983 and from 1987 to 1989 he studied at the Pontifical University of St. Thomas (Angelicum) in Rome, where he obtained a license in spiritual theology and then a doctorate in moral theology. In the mid-1980s he was a formator of Dominican friars in Kraków as the assistant Student Master, and then again from 1990 to 1994 as the Student Master. Beginning in 1984 he was also a professor of moral theology in the Dominican House of Studies in Kraków. In 1994 he was appointed an invited professor of moral theology at the Pontifical University of St. Thomas in Rome. He has continued teaching at the Angelicum until today, and he has given some lectures in Kraków on a sporadic basis over the years.

From 1998 to 2005 he was a member of the General Council of the Dominican Order, first as the Socius of the Master of the

Order for Central and Eastern Europe, and then as the Socius for the Intellectual Life of the Order in 2002–2005. In 2005, Pope Benedict XVI appointed him the Theologian of the Papal Household. Fr. Giertych is also a consultor of the Congregation for the Doctrine of the Faith, a consultor of the Congregation for Causes of Saints, a member of the Pontifical Committee for Eucharistic Congresses, the Pontifical Academy of St. Thomas Aquinas, and of the Pontifical Academy of Theology.